THE ART OF FLIGHT

A Celebration of a Century of Aeronautical Achievement

First published in Great Britain in 2015 by AgustaWestland, Lysander Road, Yeovil, Somerset BA20 2YB

www.agustawestland.com

Acknowledgements

AgustaWestland wishes to thank:

The Guild of Aviation Artists for their valuable support from the outset of this project.

The individual artists who submitted more paintings for consideration than were able to be published.

The Fleet Air Arm Museum, the Museum of Army Flying, the Royal Air Force Museum, the Defence Academy of the United Kingdom and the Officers Messes from all three UK Armed Forces for their help in sourcing additional material.

Every effort has been made to ensure the accuracy of the facts and figures in the book and all details are correct as at 1st January 2015. Aircraft production numbers refer only to new-build aircraft unless otherwise stated.

ISBN: 978-0-9932444-0-7

Written by AgustaWestland External Relations, Communication and Institutional Affairs

Printed by AgustaWestland CS&T UK Product Support and Engineering Multimedia Services Department

Bound by Remous Ltd

Contents

'The Ride Back to Bastion'

"After a Combat Logistic Patrol I hitched a ride back to Camp Bastion in a British Army Lynx."
Anthony Cowland FGAvA Afghanistan 2010

Art and design have always worked closely together and it is often said in aviation that "if it looks right it probably is right". Since Leonardo da Vinci the concept of flight has always remained in the province of the visionaries, dreamers, philosophers and artists - the stuff of legend. Long before engineers and scientists turn dreams into reality, artists have fearlessly stepped in to attempt to portray the seemingly impossible. Even after the dream becomes reality, all man's endeavours are on record in the work of artists, who can bring them to life in a way not achievable by mere words or photographs.

It is for this reason that art has been chosen to play its part in the celebration of the Westland centenary. In 1915 the Westland Aircraft Works in Yeovil opened to contribute its specialised local skills to the nation's war effort. Since then, the company has continued to design and manufacture aircraft with a boldness and spirit of innovation that have added to the legends of the aviation world. Many of the aircraft have been experimental – some successful, some not. But all deserve their place in this gallery of achievement brought together into a unique book that records every type of aeroplane and helicopter produced by Westland and AgustaWestland in the United Kingdom since 1915.

This book, created in partnership with The Guild of Aviation Artists whose members have generated the majority of the works of art, tells and illustrates the story of accomplished designers, of a highly skilled workforce and fearless flight test crews. It also celebrates the bravery of both the military and civil operators who have flown the aircraft across the world.

Daniele Romiti

Daniele Romiti
AgustaWestland Chief Executive Officer

Westland is one of the oldest aircraft manufacturers in the world and celebrates its centenary in 2015. The 100 year history of Westland, now AgustaWestland, is a long and rich one and in many ways reflective of the character of its aircraft: manifestly variable, often soaring to great heights, adaptable, interesting and always pushing the boundaries of the possible. This book is a celebration of that history, from 1915 to 2015, expressed through a unique and inspiring collection of paintings and images of its aircraft through the decades, beginning with the Short 184 and closing the century with the AW189.

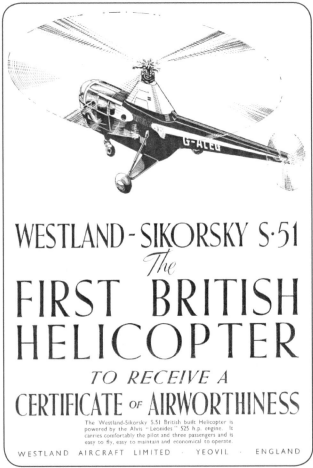

The Westland story began in 1915 when a group of skilled engineers from a Somerset agricultural engine maker called Petters Ltd began manufacturing aircraft in Yeovil. It was just a year after the start of World War I and defence materiel was running short. Petters Ltd responded to future Prime Minister Lloyd George's call on behalf of the Government for British industry to step up and aid the war effort and accepted its first contract from the Admiralty to make 12 Short 184 seaplanes for the Royal Navy. At that pivotal point in history, Westland Aircraft Works was born and so too was the relationship with the UK Armed Forces, commencing a century of customer service that is still going strong today.

Westland Aircraft Works, named after the land west of Yeovil where the first production sheds were sited, successfully delivered the first order and this was quickly followed up by further contracts for landplanes. Over 900 aircraft were manufactured for the UK Armed Forces at Westland during the First World War, including the Sopwith 1½ Strutter, the Airco DH9, DH9A and the Vickers Vimy bomber. By 1918 Westland had become a major aircraft company with its own airfield, fully established on the outskirts of Yeovil.

Despite a very active and innovative design department at Yeovil, the market in the interwar years proved more difficult, as there was a considerable drop off in demand. However, the Westland Wapiti was used worldwide by the RAF during this period and, significantly, in 1933 a Westland aircraft was the first to fly over the summit of Mount Everest, a feat which contributed both to the advancement of geographical knowledge as well as the development of pressurised aircraft cockpits.

World War II saw the Lysander, used by the Special Operations Executive, become one of the company's most iconic aircraft. During the Battle of Britain, Westland became an important centre for the repair and manufacture of Spitfires and also the main source of Seafires (the naval variant). Over 2000 Spitfires and Seafires were built in Yeovil.

Towards the end of the 1940s and into the 1950s the company took the decision to specialise in helicopters and negotiated a long-term agreement to build Sikorsky designs under licence. The Sikorsky S-51 was the first helicopter to be produced, known as the Westland Dragonfly. It was followed by the S-55 (Westland Whirlwind) and the S-58 (Westland Wessex). The last fixed wing aircraft to be produced at Yeovil was, in 1948, the Wyvern naval strike fighter. It was the end of an era. During its first 30 years, Westland had produced over 5500 fixed wing aircraft.

In 1960 the entire British aircraft industry underwent major restructuring and so did Westland which acquired Bristol Helicopters, Fairey Aviation and Saunders-Roe to become Westland Helicopters, Britain's one and only helicopter company. Meanwhile, the relationship with Sikorsky continued with the adaptation of the SH-3D to produce the Westland Sea King. Westland and Agusta worked together for the first time in 1965 when Westland produced 250 Bell 47G Sioux for the British Army under licence from the Italian company.

In a more collaborative landscape, Westland worked closely with the French firm Sud Aviation (later Aérospatiale) to produce the Lynx, Puma and Gazelle helicopters, many of which were destined for the UK Armed Forces and used extensively during the troubles in Northern Ireland from the late 1960s into the 21st century.

By the 1980s Westland had built up considerable experience in maritime helicopter design and at this time Agusta and Westland joined forces again with a venture known as EH Industries, producing the EH101, a new large helicopter replacement for the Sea King, known by the Royal Navy as the Merlin. Westland was by now the dominant supplier of helicopters to the UK Armed Forces, in particular during the Falklands War. In the 1970s the Lynx came into service with the British Army and Royal Navy. It was also used in 1986 to obtain the Helicopter World Speed Record which still stands today. In 1987 the engineering company GKN became a major shareholder in the Westland Group alongside UTC.

The early 1990s were marked by a period of change. In 1994, GKN bought the UTC shares and launched a successful takeover bid for Westland. The major programme was the Apache, built under licence from McDonnell Douglas (later Boeing), which were delivered to the British Army from 2000.

In 2001, Agusta and Westland became a single company known as Agustawestland. In 2004, GKN sold its 50% stake to the Finmeccanica group. The company initially focused on providing aircraft for UOR (Urgent Operational Requirements) in Iraq and Afghanistan, including the upgraded Lynx Mk9A.

One hundred years after the establishment of the Yeovil site, AgustaWestland is now involved in the production of the latest addition to the AW Family of helicopters, the AW189, to provide Search and Rescue aircraft for the UK. This marks a significant shift from purely military aircraft manufacture in the UK to a mixture of military and civil aircraft. In fact, the AW189 brings the number of different aircraft types made in Yeovil to more than 60 and the number of airframes built in the UK since 1915 to around 8700.

Looking forward to the next 100 years, the company continues to expand its commercial scope. On a world scale, the enterprise that started on farmland in South Somerset now stands tall as a pillar of the global aerospace industry, designing and building the most technologically advanced rotary wing aircraft in the world.

Short 184 (1915)

'Boys From Ark Royal'

Artist: Barry K Barnes GAvA

Designed by Short Brothers Ltd as a torpedo carrying seaplane, the Short 184 was the first aircraft to be built at the Westland Aircraft Works. Westland was formed in 1915 on the western edge of Yeovil, following a contract to build 12 seaplanes between Petters Ltd and the Admiralty. The first aircraft was completed by December 1915 and delivered to the Royal Navy in January 1916, by rail to the River Hamble, for final assembly and test. A Westland-built Short 184 distinguished itself with the fleet at the Battle of Jutland, being the first aircraft to have taken part in reconnaissance during a naval battle. The same aircraft was stored in the Imperial War Museum during World War II but was damaged by bombing. Only the cockpit and engine installation were saved and these are on display in the Fleet Air Arm Museum at RNAS Yeovilton, Somerset.

The painting depicts HMS Ark Royal, which was the Royal Navy's first purpose-built aircraft carrier, with her complement of Short 184s. She served in the Mediterranean and Aegean Sea throughout World War I.

First flight:	January 1916
Span:	63 ft 6 in/19.36 m
Length:	40 ft 7 in/12.38 m
Max weight:	5,100 lb/2,313 kg
Max level speed:	65 knots/121 km/h
Power plant:	One 225 hp/168 kW Sunbeam inline
Built by Westland:	12

HMS Empress, a former cross channel steamer converted to a seaplane carrier, received three Short 166 aircraft in October 1916, including two built by Westland (9754 and 9755). This aircraft was similar in appearance but smaller than the Short 184. They were used for anti-submarine patrols in the north Aegean, 9754 being replaced by another Westland-built Short 166 (9758) in November. By January 1917 these had all been transferred elsewhere in the Mediterranean. Westland was tasked with modifying the structure to allow bombs to be carried, with the modification activity being the first design work ever undertaken by Westland. A total of 20 were built at Yeovil.

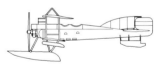

First flight:	July 1916
Span:	57 ft 3 in/17.45 m
Length:	40 ft 7 in/12.38 m
Max weight:	4,580 lb/2,077 kg
Max level speed:	56 knots/105 km/h
Power plant:	One 200 hp/149 kW Salmson radial
Built by Westland:	20

Sopwith 1½ Strutter (1916)

'Dual in the Clouds'

Artist: Paul Crocker

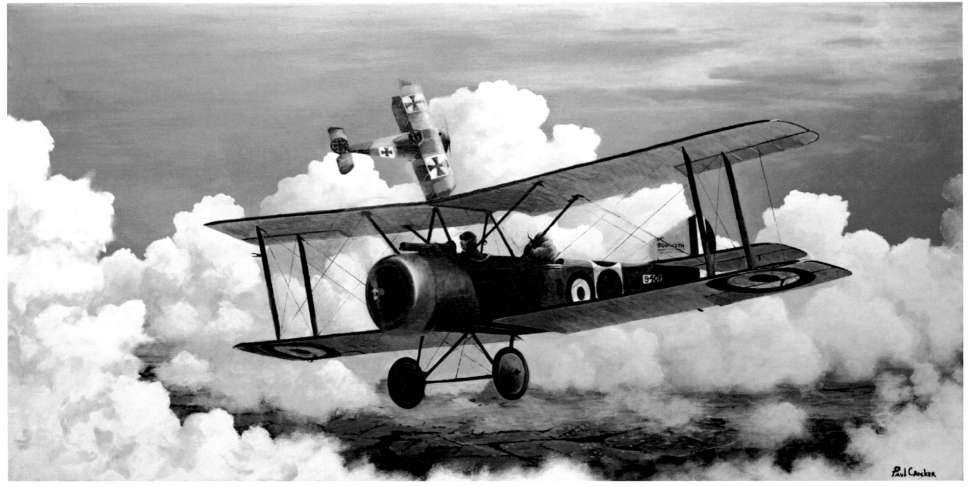

Here, a Sopwith 1½ Strutter (9407 of 3 Naval Wing) is depicted in late 1916 defending itself from a circling Fokker D.II. A total of 125 of these well-established fighter and bomber aircraft were built under licence from the Sopwith Aviation Company by Westland, destined for the Royal Naval Air Service. One hundred two seat fighters and 25 single seat bombers were constructed at Yeovil.

First flight:	Autumn 1916
Span:	33 ft 6 in/10.21 m
Length:	25 ft 3 in/7.70 m
Max weight:	2,150 lb/975 kg
Max level speed:	87 knots/161 km/h
Power plant:	One 130 hp/97 kW Clerget rotary
Built by Westland:	125

WESTLAND 1915-2015

AgustaWestland
A Finmeccanica Company

The DH4 was designed by Geoffrey de Havilland for Airco. The DH4/DH9 series of aircraft were used extensively over the Western Front for reconnaissance, artillery spotting and bombing. Westland produced over 140 DH4s, with various engine installations, during the first half of 1917. One problem with the aircraft was the distance between the pilot and observer which made communication very difficult, reducing its effectiveness in combat.

First Flight:	April 1917
Span:	42 ft 4 in/12.92 m
Length:	30 ft 8 in/9.35 m
Max weight:	3,466 lb/1,572 kg
Max level speed:	103 knots/192 km/h
Power plant:	One 230 hp/172 kW Siddeley Puma or one 250 hp/186 kW Rolls-Royce Eagle III
Built by Westland:	142

AgustaWestland
A Finmeccanica Company

WESTLAND 1915-2015

Airco DH9 (1917)

'Duxford's DH9'

Artist: David Scrutton AGAvA

Intended by de Havilland to be an improvement on the DH4, the DH9 included the modification of the cockpit layout bringing the two crew much closer together. However, because of problems with the Siddeley Puma engine which delivered only 230hp instead of the expected 300hp, the DH9's performance was inferior to that of the DH4. A barrel of Somerset cider was often used to ballast these aircraft on solo flights. The production of the DH9 formed the main part of Westland's output during 1917.

First Flight:	1917
Span:	42 ft 4 in/12.92 m
Length:	30 ft 8 in/9.30 m
Max weight:	3,325 lb/1,508 kg
Max level speed:	96 knots/177 km/h
Power plant:	One 230 hp/172 kW Siddeley Puma or one 250 hp/186 kW Rolls-Royce Eagle III
Built by Westland:	Approx 250 (full order not completed)

The N1B was Westland's first attempt to design a complete aircraft in response to a requirement for a small shipborne seaplane for the Royal Naval Air Service. The aircraft performed well in the official flight trials at the Isle of Grain in October 1917, but in the end, the contract was won by the Sopwith Baby. However, the aircraft represented a significant step forward in Westland's development.

First flight:	August 1917
Span:	31 ft 4 in/9.54 m
Length:	25 ft 5 in/7.76 m
Max weight:	1,978 lb /897 kg
Max level speed:	94 knots/174 km/h
Power plant:	One 150 hp/112 kW Bentley BR1 rotary
Built by Westland:	2

Airco DH9A (1918)

'Travellers'

Artist: Anthony Cowland FGAvA

Shown here after a desert landing in North Africa, the DH9A was an important aircraft for Westland, which was entrusted to execute the considerable redesign of the DH9 to fit a US-built Liberty engine. This significantly improved its climb performance and ceiling. Westland subsequently became the main manufacturer for the type, producing approximately 355 aircraft. The design capability at Westland thus became well-established. The DH9A provided a basis for much of the company's post-war work and led to the design of the Westland Wapiti.

First flight:	March 1918
Span:	45 ft 10 in/13.97 m
Length:	29 ft 10 in/9.07 m
Max weight:	2,770 lb/1,256 kg
Max level speed:	104 knots/193 km/h
Power plant:	One 400 hp/298 kW Liberty 12 or one 375 hp/280 kW Rolls-Royce Eagle VIII or one 450 hp/336 kW Napier Lion
Built by Westland:	Approx 355

Offered by Westland against a War Office requirement for a single seat fighter in April 1918, the Wagtail was designed with the ABC Wasp seven cylinder 170 hp engine. During 1918 the Wagtail was sent to Martlesham Heath for trials alongside the Sopwith Snail, also fitted with the Wasp. Unfortunately the Wasp was not a successful engine, hence the title of the painting, as the aircraft were not only competing with each other but with their engines. In the end, probably due to the impending armistice, the Wagtail was not accepted for production. Five prototypes were built and used for work with experimental equipment and engines.

First flight:	April 1918
Span:	23 ft 2 in/7.06 m
Length:	18 ft 11 in/5.77 m
Max weight:	1,330 lb/603 kg
Max level speed:	109 knots/201 km/h
Power plant:	One 170 hp/127 kW ABC Wasp
Built by Westland.	5

Westland Weasel (1918)

'Weasel v Badger v Dragonfly'

Artist: James Field AGAvA

In a very similar scenario to the Westland Wagtail, the Westland Weasel was to be defeated by its ABC Dragonfly nine cylinder engine. The Weasel was a two seat fighter designed to succeed the Bristol F2b Fighter at the end of World War I. However, the failure of the power plant and the ending of the war meant that further development was very limited. The Weasel, along with the Bristol Badger and the Austin Greyhound, would have struggled to show their potential in fighter trials when so badly handicapped by their engines. Designed by Robert Bruce and Arthur Davenport, two key figures in the early years of Westland, the Weasel was offered as a two seat fighter reconnaissance aircraft but was not selected for service. However, it carried some early innovations such as electrical heating and oxygen equipment and all four prototypes were used for engine test work.

First flight:	Late 1918
Span:	35 ft 6 in/10.82 m
Length:	24 ft 10 in/7.57 m
Max weight:	3,071 lb/1,393 kg
Max level speed:	103 knots/209 km/h
Power plant:	One 320 hp/239 kW ABC Dragonfly
Built by Westland:	4

WESTLAND 1915-2015

AgustaWestland
A Finmeccanica Company

Prior to the war ending, the newly-formed RAF was planning a major bombing assault on Germany. In order to sustain this, several smaller companies undertook to produce these large machines and Westland received an order for 75 Vickers Vimy twin engine bombers. Being a large aircraft by the standards of the time, the company needed larger facilities. The 'Vimy Hanger' was built at Yeovil with a single unsupported span of 140 feet – the largest of its kind in Britain at that time. It remains in use today. In the end 25 Vimys were built by Westland for the RAF and were used for post-war long distance flights, so it is fitting that this painting depicts the aircraft flying alongside the pyramids in Egypt.

First flight:	1919
Span:	68 ft 0 in/20.73 m
Length:	43 ft 6 in/13.27 m
Max weight:	12,500 lb/5,670 kg
Max level speed:	89 knots/166 km/h
Power plant:	Two 360 hp/268 kW Rolls-Royce Eagle VIII
Built by Westland:	25

AgustaWestland
A Finmeccanica Company

WESTLAND 1915-2015

Westland Limousine I & II (1919)

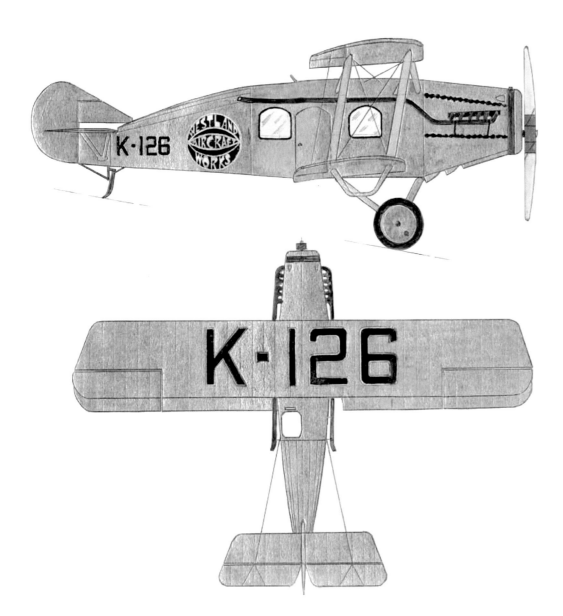

First flight:	July 1919
Span:	38 ft 2 in/11.51 m
Length:	27 ft 9 in/8.46 m
Max weight:	3,383 lb/1,535 kg
Max level speed:	78 knots/145 km/h
Power plant:	One 275 hp/205 kW Rolls Royce Falcon III
Built by Westland:	1 (I) and 5 (II)

With the cessation of hostilities in November 1918, Arthur Davenport, promoted by the Petter brothers to be Westland's Chief Designer, was already exploring the requirements of the post war civil air services. Instead of modifying an existing military aircraft Davenport boldly produced a completely new design with the declared intention of combining all the best points of a high class motor car with the advantage of the speed of an aeroplane.

The outcome was the Limousine I, a single engine biplane of wooden construction with fabric and wood covering. The passengers were in an enclosed cabin, the pilot sat in the port rear of the four seats. His seat was raised to enable his head to be above the cabin roof. Westland Aircraft Works described the aircraft as follows:

"The interior of the cabin is upholstered in the style characteristic of the very finest of motor-car bodies, the seats are extremely comfortable, and there is plenty of leg room. Conversation can be carried out with ease, and although there are no draughts, there is no trace of odour from the engine."

The Limousine II was built and used for both passenger carrying and mail services between Croydon, Paris and Brussels until withdrawal from service in 1923.

Both the Limousine I and II proved to be too small to operate economically and, inspired by the Air Ministry Commercial Aircraft Competition, Robert Bruce and Arthur Davenport decided to build a much larger six passenger version, designated Limousine III. Although it won first prize of £7500 it failed to achieve commercial success and only two examples were built. One (G-EARV) was bought by Sidney Cotton in 1920 for operation by Aerial Survey Company (Newfoundland) Ltd. It was used for seal and fishery spotting and also carried mail and passengers until the end of 1923. The aircraft was fitted with skis and the painting shows members of the company staff chasing after the skidding aircraft to help bring the 'Wayward Westland' to a halt, with the hapless pilot out of the cockpit and sitting on the fuselage.

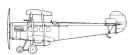

First flight:	June 1920
Span:	54 ft 0 in/16.46 m
Length:	33 ft 6 in/10.21 m
Max weight:	3,823 lb/1,734 kg
Max level speed:	102 knots/190 km/h
Power plant:	One 450 hp/336 kW Napier Lion
Built by Westland:	2

AgustaWestland
A Finmeccanica Company

WESTLAND 1915-2015

Westland Walrus (1921)

'Pre-Flight Check'

Artist: Paul Crocker

WESTLAND WALRUS 423 FLIGHT 1423/4 BY Paul Crocker

First flight:	February 1921
Span:	45 ft 10 in/13.97 m
Length:	30 ft 0 in/9.14 m
Max weight:	4,994 lb/2,265 kg
Max level speed:	108 knots/200 km/h
Power plant:	One 450 hp/336 kW Napier Lion II
Built by Westland:	36

The Walrus was a three seat spotter-reconnaissance aircraft based upon an extensively modified DH9A airframe. Although it was originally designed for use with the Royal Navy's new aircraft carriers it ultimately went into service with the RAF. Westland's Erecting Shop foreman, Harry Dalwood, was taken along on the first flight by the Chief Test Pilot, Captain Arthur Stuart Keep. During the flight the Walrus's nose dropped severely due to a problem with the throttle, so Dalwood climbed out onto the rear fuselage to enable Keep to land safely.

The contract for the RAF came at a very welcome time for Westland, making it possible for the company to prepare for the less lucrative peacetime years ahead. A total of 36 aircraft were produced, remaining in service until 1925.

AgustaWestland
A Finmeccanica Company

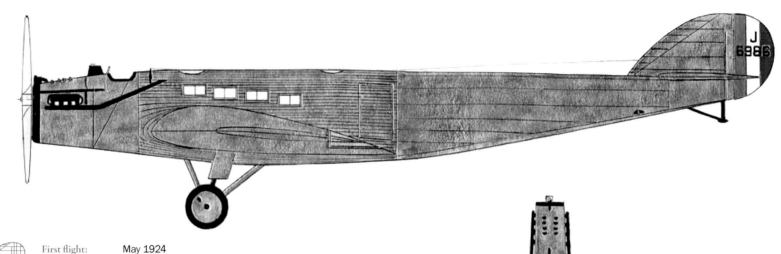

First flight:	May 1924
Span:	69 ft 6 in/21.18 m
Length:	56 ft 0 in/17.07 m
Max weight:	6,900 lb/3,130 kg estimated
Max level speed:	102 knots/190 km/h estimated
Power plant:	One 450 hp/336 kW Napier Lion
Built by Westland:	1

In the post-war years the Air Ministry was interested in the theories of a Russian inventor, Nicolas Woyevodsky, whose idea of the perfect aeroplane was that the fuselage and wings should be in the form of a continuous aerofoil, with external wing bracing eliminated, rather like the modern conception of the "flying wing."

Westland's response was the Dreadnought. It was an all-metal monoplane, distinctly futuristic in its silver paint. Its construction methods were also ahead of the times, including drawn metal channelling and corrugated metal panels, similar to the modern "stressed skin" method of manufacture.

The aircraft marked a turning point in Westland's aerodynamic design process. On its first flight, piloted by Captain Keep, the Dreadnought stalled and crashed immediately after take off. Captain Keep's life was saved by company nurse Sister Thomas, but he tragically lost both legs in the incident.

The Petters Monthly News of May 1924 stated:

'It is unfortunately true that the men who possess the courage and skill which enables them to undertake pioneer work are always exposed to the dangers which accompany their work. Practically all the advantages of civilisation which we enjoy have been obtained for us at the cost of suffering on the part of those who first made the venture into unknown fields.'

The Dreadnought design was abandoned, although the incident led to Westland installing a more powerful wind tunnel to improve aerodynamic accuracy. Captain Keep remained with the company, retiring in 1935 as Works Manager.

Westland Woodpigeon I & II (1924)

'Westland Woodpigeon at Lympne 1924'   *Artist: Martin Perman AGAvA*

The little Woodpigeon was built as a response to the Air Ministry's Light Aeroplane Competition of 1924. Westland also produced a monoplane entry, the Widgeon, which proved superior and as a consequence only two Woodpigeon prototypes were built, the second of which was larger in an attempt to improve the performance.

First flight:	17th September 1924
Span:	27 ft 0 in/8.23 m
Length:	20 ft 9 in/6.32 m
Max weight:	885 lb/401 kg
Max level speed:	61 knots/113 km/h
Power plant:	One 32 hp/24 kW Bristol Cherub III (I), one 60 hp/45 kW Anzani radial (II)
Built by Westland:	2

The Widgeon was Westland's second entry in the 1924 competition, built to ensure that consideration should be given to a monoplane configuration. The trials aircraft was unfortunately damaged in the course of the competition and this lead to the Widgeon II. The Widgeon III was based on experience gained from the I and II and it was developed to provide a light aircraft in quantity for the private ownership market.

Widgeons were sold to South Africa, Canada and Australia and also achieved success on the sporting scene. The type appeared with a number of different engines and proved to be very popular among more affluent private owners.

First flight:	22nd September 1924
Span:	30 ft 8 in/9.35 m (I&II) 36 ft 4½ in/11.09 m (III)
Length:	21 ft 0 in/6.4 m (I&II) 23 ft 5 in/7.14 m (III)
Max weight:	1150 lb/522 kg (I&II) 935 lb/424 kg (III)
Max level speed:	75-95 knots/138-177 km/h
Power plants:	One 35 hp/26k W Blackburn Thrush or one Armstrong Siddeley Genet (I&II), one 75 hp/75 kW Armstrong Siddeley Genet II or one 85 hp/63 kW ABC Hornet or one 85 hp/63 kW ADC Cirrus II or one 90 hp/67 kW ADC Cirrus II or one 100 hp/75 kW de Havilland Gipsy I or one 105 hp/78 kW Cirrus Hermes I or one 120 hp/89 kW Cirrus Hermes II (III)
Built by Westland:	26

AgustaWestland
A Finmeccanica Company

WESTLAND 1915-2015

Westland Yeovil (1925)

'Westland Yeovil'

Artist: Brian How AGAvA

Air Ministry Specification 26/23 called for a two seat long range day bomber for the Royal Air Force competed for by Bristol Aeroplane Company Ltd, H.G. Hawker Engineering, Handley Page Ltd and Westland Aircraft Works. Three Westland Yeovil prototypes were built and, although all four competing types were remarkably similar in appearance and performance, it was the Hawker Horsley's ability to carry the heaviest bomb load and a torpedo that won the selection.

The three Westland aircraft remained in flying condition for a number of years because their good handling and performance characteristics made them excellent for research and test flying a wide range of equipment.

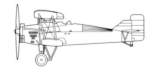

First flight:	June 1925
Span:	59 ft 6 in/18.14 m
Length:	36 ft 0 in/11.23 m
Max weight:	7,550 lb/3,425 kg
Max level speed:	104 knots/193 km/h
Power plant:	One 650 hp/485 kW Rolls-Royce Condor III
Built by Westland:	3

AgustaWestland
A Finmeccanica Company

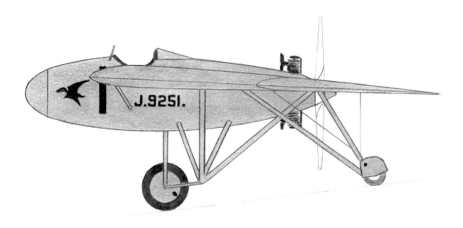

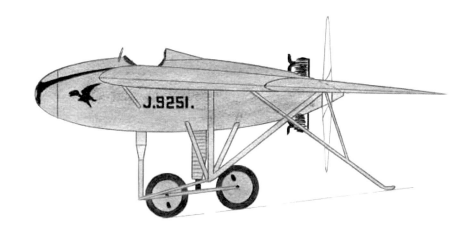

First flight:	June 1926
Span:	45 ft 6 in/13.87 m
Length:	17 ft 0 in/5.18 m
Max weight:	900 lb/408 kg
Max level speed:	61 knots/113 km/h
Power plant:	One 32 hp/48 kW Bristol Cherub III (IA), one 70 hp/52 kW Armstrong Siddeley Genet (IB)
Built by Westland:	1

The Pterodactyl I was the first of a series of experimental designs undertaken by Westland working with Captain Geoffrey Hill to investigate the handling qualities of tailless aircraft.

Starting out as a single seat glider, it incorporated a control system consisting of wing tip 'elevons' and trailing edge flaps/rudders. In the course of an extensive flight programme it was converted into a two seat powered research aircraft and a viable control system was demonstrated. A single prototype was built, which is now on display in the Science Museum in London.

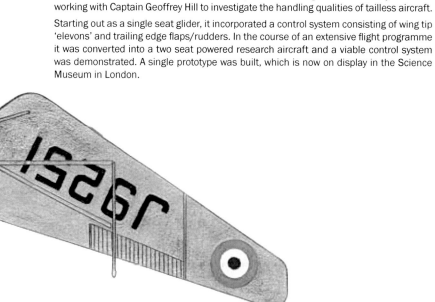

Westland Wizard I & II (1926)

'Spell of Elegance'

Artist: Patrick Sadler AGAvA

Designed during 'out of office hours' by a small group of employees from the Design Office, the Wizard was intended as a fast monoplane racer. Robert Bruce and Arthur Davenport supported the project and it progressed to construction. Piloted by Laurence Openshaw, the original prototype was badly damaged during an emergency landing and it was rebuilt with an all-metal fuselage and provision for armament. Living up to its ambitions, the Westland Wizard exhibited speed and a remarkable rate of climb. The Air Ministry demonstrated interest in the Wizard and invested in further modifications and improvements, however the type was eventually rejected through service prejudice against the monoplane configuration. The image shows the remarkably clean lines of the Wizard II with the supercharged Rolls-Royce engine – one of the most elegant of Westland designs.

First flight:	November 1926
Span:	39 ft 6 in/12.04 m
Length:	26 ft 10 in/8.18 m
Max weight:	3,2750 lb/1,486 kg
Max level speed:	163 knots/303 km/h
Power plant:	One 490 hp/365 kW Rolls-Royce F XI (I), one 500 hp/373 kW Rolls-Royce F XIS (II)
Built by Westland:	1

WESTLAND 1915-2015

AgustaWestland
A Finmeccanica Company

In contrast to the elegant Wizard, the Westbury was built in response to Air Ministry requirement 4/24 which called for a large heavily-armed twin engine fighter. An important part of the requirement was the need to carry two 37mm cannon, for which considerable structural strength was necessary. Other contenders for the contract failed to meet this requirement, but the whole concept was eventually discarded by the Ministry and the Westbury did not proceed beyond the prototype stage.

This decision, which coincided with the financial slump around 1927-28, reflected the parlous state of the British aircraft industry. At one time the manpower in the Westland Aircraft Works dropped to half-a-dozen foremen and a dozen men.

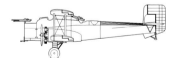

First flight:	1927
Span:	68 ft 0 in/20.73 m
Length:	43 ft 5 in/13.23 m
Max weight:	7,877 lb/3,573 kg
Max level speed:	109 knots/201 km/h
Power plant:	Two 450 hp/336 kW Bristol Jupiter VI
Built by Westland:	2

- BARRY K BARNES -

The Wapiti holds a special place in Westland's history. Not only did it achieve production in significant numbers but its sales and production took place during a time when most areas of the British aircraft industry were suffering the effects of the recession. There can be little doubt that without the Wapiti, the company would probably have been unable to continue functioning as an aircraft manufacturer.

The Wapiti was produced in response to Air Ministry Specification 26/27 calling for a DH9A replacement which also specified a great deal of commonality. As a DH9A design authority, Westland was well-placed to respond to this. The Wapiti was selected against seven other contenders to become the mainstay of operations as a general purpose aircraft for the RAF for the next ten years. There were even a few in use at the beginning of World War II.

The aircraft underwent continuous modification during its long service life, mostly incorporating a range of engines and more extensive use of metal components. There were eight distinctive versions of the aircraft flown before production ceased in 1932.

100

WESTLAND 1915-2015

AgustaWestland

A Finmeccanica Company

First flight:	7th March 1927
Span:	46 ft 5 in/14.15 m
Length:	31 ft 8 in/9.65 m
Max weight:	5,400 lb/2,449 kg
Max level speed:	122 knots/225 km/h
Power plant:	One 480 hp/358 kW Bristol Jupiter VIIIF (IIA), one 550 hp/ 410 kW Armstrong Siddeley Panther (IB, South Africa), one 490 hp/365 kW Armstrong Siddeley Jaguar VI (III, South Africa), numerous other power plants fitted experimentally.
Built by Westland:	558, plus 27 built under licence in South Africa

Westland Witch (1928)

'Testing the Witch'

Artist: Martin Perman AGAvA

Air Ministry Specification 23/25 called for a two seat day bomber. Four companies responded with proposals including Westland's entry of the Witch which included an innovative 'on board' bomb load. The requirement was eventually dropped and only a single prototype was built. This painting visualises a test flight in the late 1920s.

First flight:	30th January 1928
Span:	61 ft 0 in/18.59 m
Length:	37 ft 8 in/11.48 m
Max weight:	6,050 lb/2,744 kg
Max level speed:	122 knots/225 km/h
Power plant:	One 480 hp/358 kW Bristol Jupiter VIIIF
Built by Westland:	1

The Interceptor was a bold attempt to introduce a monoplane configuration in the face of the official line which favoured biplanes. It was offered in response to Air Ministry Specification F20/27 for a daylight fighter capable of high speed and rate of climb. Sadly, following rigorous testing at Martlesham Heath, it was rejected by the RAF together with its two contenders, the Vickers Jockey and the de Havilland DH77. All three monoplane designs exhibited unsatisfactory performance and handling characteristics.

Nonetheless, these monoplane prototypes held a place in fighter design history in an attempt to depart from the trend of that time. The sole Westland Interceptor continued to fly until 1935.

Subsequently, the superior Hawker Fury biplane of 1931 was adopted as the design put into service to meet this Air Ministry requirement. The Fury was later developed into the famous Hurricane, a monoplane.

First flight:	August 1928
Span:	38 ft 0 in/11.58 m
Length:	25 ft 4 in/7.73 m
Max weight:	3,325 lb/1,508 kg
Max level speed:	167 knots/309 km/h
Power plant:	One 420 hp/313 kW Bristol Jupiter VII
Built by Westland:	1

Kai Choi XI 2014

AgustaWestland
A Finmeccanica Company

WESTLAND 1915-2015

The Westland IV was the company's first attempt to produce a light passenger transport for the civil market. The three engine configuration was adopted to increase safety. Trials with the prototype were successful and there was interest from the light aviation fraternity. A number of improvements were proposed, leading to the similarly configured Wessex.

The sketch shows G-AAGW, the second Westland IV which was later re-engined to become a Westland Wessex which flew with Imperial Airways.

First flight:	22nd February 1929
Span:	57 ft 6 in/17.53 m
Length:	37 ft 6 in/11.43 m
Max weight:	5,500 lb/2,495 kg
Max level speed:	94 knots/174 km/h
Power plant:	Three 105 hp/78 kW ADC Cirrus Hermes I
Built by Westland:	2

Success with the Westland IV led to the construction of the Wessex, which incorporated a number of structural improvements and was capable of carrying up to six passengers in comfort. More powerful engines were fitted which offered increased performance, reliability and safety. The very competitive de Havilland Dragon and Rapide range of airliners entered the market at about this time, with the result that only a limited number of Wessex were sold before production ceased.

In 1933 G-AAGW was chartered by the Great Western Railway to fly a twice daily service on the Plymouth Teignmouth Cardiff route with the interior upholstered in the style of a first class railway carriage. The flight was three hours faster than travel by rail because of the direct route across the Bristol Channel.

Artist: *John Dimond GAvA*

First flight:	May 1930
Span:	57 ft 6 in/17.53 m
Length:	38 ft 0 in/11.58 m
Max weight:	6,300 lb/2,858 kg
Max level speed:	106 knots/196 km/h
Power plant:	Three 140 hp/104 kW Armstrong Siddeley Genet Major IA
Built by Westland:	8

AgustaWestland
A Finmeccanica Company

WESTLAND 1915-2015

'*Westland C.O.W Gun Fighter*'

Artist: Kai Choi AGAvA

The C.O.W. (Coventry Ordnance Works) Gun Fighter first flew at the end of 1930.

It was a development of the Westland Interceptor aircraft; this was Westland's response to Air Ministry Specification F29/27 which required an upward firing C.O.W. gun to be fitted.

The C.O.W. gun was a 37mm cannon developed during World War I. This gun was configured on the Westland design to fire at an upward direction of 55 degrees towards an intended target from below. Due to unsatisfactory results from earlier trials the concept was abandoned. The recoil force of an upward firing cannon of such a calibre when fired would certainly have had an effect upon the directional control of the aircraft.

Ironically the idea was later adopted with considerable success by the Luftwaffe in World War II on their night fighters. This upwards firing installation became known as 'Schräge Musik' (Jazz Music).

First flight:	December 1930
Span:	40 ft 10 in/12.45 m
Length:	29 ft 10 in/9.09 m
Max weight:	3,885 lb/1,792 kg
Max level speed:	160 knots/296 km/h
Power plant:	One 485 hp/362 kW Bristol Mercury IIIA
Built by Westland:	1

The work carried out with the Pterodactyl I showed sufficient promise to make the construction of a more sophisticated tailless aircraft a viable proposition. The Pterodactyl IV was capable of carrying a crew of three in an enclosed cabin.

Trials demonstrated a high level of control and manoeuvrability coupled with good handling characteristics. It was also possible to vary the wing sweep in flight. Although the decision was taken not to develop the Pterodactyl into a production civil aircraft it was to prove itself as a valuable source of data as a tailless research vehicle for the small but growing Westland design team.

First flight:	March 1931
Span:	44 ft 4 in/13.51 m
Length:	19 ft 6 in/5.94 m
Max weight:	2,100 lb/953 kg
Max level speed:	98 knots/182 km/h
Power plant:	One 120 hp/89 kW de Havilland Gipsy III
Built by Westland:	1

Westland PV3 and Westland PV6 (1931)   *'First Over Everest'*   *Artist: Michael Turner FGAvA (President)*

Originally designed as a torpedo bomber for the Royal Navy, the PV3 was based on the Wapiti. Although no orders materialised, a PV3 was acquired by the Royal Geographical Society and modified for an expedition to fly over the summit of Mount Everest (29,029 ft/ 8,848 m). PV6, which became the Westland Wallace prototype, was selected as a back-up. The aircraft were renamed as Houston-Westland and Houston-Wallace after the expedition's financier Lady Houston.

The Houston Mount Everest Expedition's goal was to prove that a British aircraft with a British crew could fly over the highest point on earth. At the same time they were to photograph and film this previously inaccessible and dangerous terrain, with a view to contributing to scientific knowledge and development. Both aircraft were modified with heating systems for cameras and crew suits, oxygen supplies, enclosed rear cabins and the Bristol Pegasus IS3 engine.

The first flight over Mount Everest was successfully completed by both aircraft on 3rd April 1933 to much acclaim in the press. A second flight, against orders, was carried out to achieve the expedition's scientific aims. The Auxiliary Air Force pilots were reprimanded for what The Times called 'a magnificent piece of insubordination' but they were subsequently awarded the Air Force Cross.

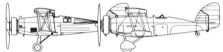

First flight:	February 1931 (PV3) 31st October 1931 (PV6)
Span:	46 ft 6 in/14.17 m
Length:	34 ft 2 in/10.41 m
Max weight:	5,600 lb/2,540 kg
Max level speed:	142 knots/262 km/h
Power plant:	One 575 hp/429 kW Bristol Jupiter XFA (Everest: One 630 hp/ 507 kW Bristol Pegasus IS3)
Built by Westland:	1 (PV3) and 1 (PV6)

As part of a programme to continue improvement of the successful Wapiti, Westland produced the PV6, which was offered to the RAF as the Westland Wallace.

The improvement was such that production orders followed, together with contracts to upgrade a number of Wapitis to Wallace standard. It later became the first aircraft in service with the RAF to feature an enclosed cockpit and cabin. Here, a 501 Squadron aircraft flies over the Clifton Suspension Bridge over the River Avon in Bristol. At the outbreak of World War II, 83 remained in service with the RAF and the Wallace served on until finally being withdrawn in December 1943.

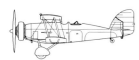

First flight:	31st October 1931
Span:	46 ft 5 in/14.15 m
Length:	34 ft 2 in/10.41 m
Max weight:	5,750 lb/2,608 kg
Max level speed:	137 knots/254 km/h
Power plant:	One 680 hp/507 kW Bristol Pegasus IV
Built by Westland:	115, plus 60 conversions from Wapiti

Westland PV7 (1933)

Artist: Kai Choi AGAvA

Intended as Westland's private venture in response to Air Ministry Specification G4/31, the PV7 was a two seat multi-role aircraft with a number of advanced design features of the time. The requirement for a bomb bay and torpedo carrying capabilities necessitated a complicated undercarriage design, similar to that on the earlier Westland Witch. The enclosed cockpit was a later refinement following earlier trials with an open cockpit configuration. No fewer than nine companies submitted designs, none of which were eventually accepted.

The unfortunate mid-air break up of the sole PV7 prototype during official RAF tests on 25th August 1934 ended the development programme prematurely. Its pilot on this occasion was Westland's own Chief Test Pilot, Harald Penrose, pictured below. This was the very first parachute escape from an enclosed aircraft cockpit.

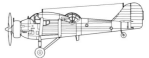

First flight:	3rd October 1933
Span:	60 ft 3 in/18.36 m
Length:	38 ft 8 in/11.79 m
Max weight:	4,515 lb/2,048 kg
Max level speed:	150 knots/278 km/h
Power plant:	One 722 hp/538 kW Bristol Pegasus III M3
Built by Westland:	1

Such was the promise of the Pterodactyl demonstrations that an order was placed for a prototype capable of development into a fighter (Air Ministry Specification F3/32).

The Pterodactyl V incorporated many of the features demonstrated by the earlier aircraft plus provision for armament. Trials at Royal Aircraft Establishment Farnborough led to the conclusion that the tailless configuration did not offer any significant improvement over conventional fighters then under development.

First flight:	May 1934
Span:	46 ft 8 in/14.22 m
Length:	22 ft 10 in/6.96 m
Max weight:	5,100 lb/2,313 kg
Max level speed:	165 knots/306 km/h
Power plant:	One 600 hp/447 kW Rolls-Royce Goshawk
Built by Westland:	1

Westland F7/30 (1934)

'The Westland F7/30'

Artist: David Calow GAvA

Air Ministry Specification F7/30 was drawn up to spur innovation in the development of high speed fighters, including the need for a "good fighting view" from the cockpit. The Westland response incorporated some interesting features which would be of great advantage for aerial combat. The engine was mounted behind the pilot and on the centre of gravity, resulting in excellent all-round visibility and the potential for good handling. The grouping of four machine guns in the nose was good practice for gun harmonisation.

Trials at Martlesham Heath showed that the handling qualities were indeed good, but the aircraft performance was poor against the specification – probably due to the biplane configuration. In the end none of the three competing aircraft met the requirement and no contract was awarded. The prototype was used for experimental flying at Yeovil and RAE Farnborough before being broken up in 1935.

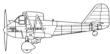

First flight:	27th March 1934
Span:	38 ft 6 in/11.73 m
Length:	29 ft 6 in/8.99 m
Max weight:	5,200 lb/2,359 kg
Max level speed:	161 knots/298 km/h
Power plant:	One 600 hp/447 kW Rolls-Royce Goshawk VIII
Built by Westland:	1

'The One that Wouldn't Fly'
Artist: Simon Milan GAvA

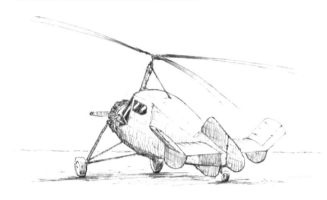

Rotor diameter:	50 ft 0 in/15.24 m
Length:	38 ft 0 in/11.58 m
Max weight:	5,000 lb/2,268 kg
Max speed:	139 knots/257 km/h (estimated)
Power:	One 600 hp/447 kW Armstrong Siddeley Panther II
Built by Westland:	1

A single prototype of this five seat autogyro was produced for Cierva, with Westland designing the fuselage and Cierva responsible for the construction of the rotor and rotor control mechanism. However, production did not progress beyond the ground running phase due to ground resonance for which no remedy could be found. It was perhaps fitting that Robert Bruce, Works and later Managing Director who had joined the company in the very earliest days in 1915, had design input into Westland's first foray into rotary-winged aircraft.

First flight:	5th February 1935
Rotor diameter:	32 ft 0 in/9.75 m
Length:	20 ft 3 in/ 6.17 m
Max weight:	1,400 lb/635 kg
Max speed:	92 knots/171 km/h
Power:	One 90 hp/67 kW Pobjoy Niagra S
Built by Westland:	1

'CL20'
Artist: Simon Milan GAvA

The CL20 was the second of two autogyros built for Cierva. Designed jointly by Cierva and Lepere, it was flown successfully at Cierva's base at Hanworth but work was stopped due to the oncoming threat of war.

AgustaWestland
A Finmeccanica Company

WESTLAND 1915-2015

The Audax was produced in large numbers, with 625 ordered for the RAF alone, of which well over half (453) were produced by sub-contractors, including Bristol, Gloster, A V Roe and Westland (42). The Audax was the main army co-operation aircraft in RAF service from 1932 until its replacement by the Westland Lysander in 1937-8. The Audax was then used for second line duties, amongst them advanced training and communication duties in Britain.

The Audax saw most active service in India where the RAF had been stripped of many modern aircraft during the first two years of the war, leaving it very vulnerable after the Japanese entry into the war in December 1941. Two squadrons were even forced to use the Audax as single seat fighters, before receiving the Curtiss Mohawk in early 1942.

The final squadrons to use the Audax were in the Indian Air Force and, remarkably, they used the Audax in its original role, as an army co-operation aircraft until January 1944.

The Hawker Hector was designed to replace the Hawker Audax as an army co-operation aircraft with a new engine and a straight wing replacing the swept back upper wing of the earlier aircraft. Despite these visual changes, the Hector was very similar to the Audax so the development and production was rapid. Hawker received orders for 178 Hectors, and despite the production switching from Hawker to Westland, all 178 were completed within 2 years by the end of 1937.

The Hector equipped seven RAF army co-operation squadrons from 1937 to 1939, when it was replaced by the Westland Lysander. The Hectors were then transferred to five squadrons of the Royal Auxiliary Air Force. In May 1940 613 Squadron RAuxAF used its Hectors in attacks on the German troops advancing through northern France, losing two aircraft during one mission near Calais. In June 1940 the squadron finished converting to the Lysander, ending the front line career of the Hector. Between 1940 and 1942 the Hector served as a glider tug, before more modern aircraft became available for that role.

First flight:	1935 (Audax), 1936 (Hector)
Span:	36 ft 11 ins /11.26 m
Length:	29 ft 9 ins/ 9.09 m
Max weight:	4,910 lb /2,227 kg
Max level speed:	161 knots/298 km/h
Power plant:	One 575 hp/429 kW Rolls-Royce Kestrel X (Audax)
	One 600 hp/447 kW Rolls-Royce Goshawk VIII (Hector)
Built by Westland:	42 (Audax), 178 (Hector)

WESTLAND 1915-2015

AgustaWestland
A Finmeccanica Company

Probably the most famous of the Westland fixed wing aircraft, the Lysander was designed in response to Air Ministry Specification A39/34 for a two seat army co-operation aircraft capable of operating from short fields or unprepared strips.

The Westland response met the specification perfectly and was ordered in large quantities, but in 1940 Lysanders fared badly against the Luftwaffe's full scale 'Blitzkreig' in France and they were withdrawn. Fourteen RAF air-sea rescue squadrons and flights were formed in 1940 and 1941, dropping dinghies to downed RAF aircrew in the English Channel.

The Lysander is best remembered for its clandestine role in carrying Special Operations Executive agents to link up with resistance movements in occupied Europe. With its high-lift, short take off and landing capabilities the Lysander could land on crude and short fields to drop off or pick up agents.

To give the necessary long range the aircraft were modified by removing all unnecessary heavy equipment, then fitted with a large drop fuel tank under the belly. A fixed ladder provided quick access to the rear cockpit. Painted black for camouflage, and usually flying by the glow of a full moon, the pilots required great navigational skills to find the landing strips marked out by a few torches, hastily lit and doused as needed.

Westland Lysander (1936)

'Secret Rendezvous'

Artist: Patricia Forrest GAvA

Production of the Lysander, the largest production of an aircraft of Westland's own design, ceased in December 1941. Worthy of note is that the first 12 were built at a fixed price of £15,189 but by the time 150 had been built this had reduced to £3,063 for each aircraft.

First flight:	15th June 1936
Span:	50 ft 0 in/15.24 m
Length:	30 ft 6 in/9.30 m
Max weight:	5,920 lb/2,685 kg
Max level speed:	199 knots/369 km/h
Power plant:	One 890 hp/664 kW Bristol Mercury VII
Built by Westland:	1,427, plus 225 in Canada under licence.

AgustaWestland
A Finmeccanica Company

With the approach of war the Air Ministry identified a need for a long range twin engine fighter against the possibility that the main air battle would be fought over the European mainland. Westland responded with the Whirlwind, a small, fast, twin engine fighter with formidable armament: four 20 mm cannon mounted in a close group in the nose. The resultant aircraft proved to be very fast and manoeuvrable, matching and, in some areas, exceeding that of the Spitfire.

As events transpired, the fall of France meant that the air battle was to be fought over Britain and the need for an aircraft such as the Whirlwind not only receded but would be a drain on resources. Further to this the Peregrine engine was at an early stage of development. The programme continued with lower priority and the Whirlwind achieved limited production as a fighter-bomber, colloquially known as the 'Whirlibomber'.

In this guise it participated in many 'Rhubarb Operations', attacking targets of opportunity such as shipping, aerodromes, bridges and, as in the painting, locomotives. This particular 'Rhubarb' was conducted by two pilots of 263 Squadron RAF, namely Flight Sergeants Proctor and Dunlop flying from RAF Warmwell.

Westland Whirlwind (1938)

Artist: Terry Akehurst

'Final Checks'

First flight:	11th October 1938
Span:	45 ft 0 in/13.72 m
Length:	32 ft 9 in/9.98 m
Max weight:	10,356 lb/4,697 kg
Max speed:	313 knots/579 km/h
Power plant:	Two 885 hp/660 kW Rolls-Royce Peregrine
Built by Westland:	116

As the nation re-armed for World War II, Yeovil was committed to production of the Lysander and Whirlwind fighter. There was some spare capacity and Westland took this up with small Spitfire contracts. By July 1940 it had already been agreed that Westland would manufacture the Spitfire, before the Supermarine factory at Southampton was totally destroyed in September of that year. As well as the main site in Yeovil, Spitfires were also worked on at dispersal sites in Ilchester, Sherborne and Martock. Westland was re-classified as a Spitfire centre and maintained spares and repairs until Castle Bromwich came online.

The first Westland-built Spitfire rose up from Yeovil on 8th July 1941 in the hands of Harald Penrose, leading to a total production of both the MkI and MkV of 685. The last Spitfire was delivered in November 1943 by which time the company was building Seafires.

Employee numbers working on the Lysander and Whirlwind was at around 2,750 in 1940 but with the additional work on Supermarine aircraft this rose to a wartime peak of 6,500. The initial cost of a Westland-built Spitfire was £6,600.

First flight:	8th July 1941
Span:	36 ft 10 in/11.23 m
Length:	29 ft 11 in/9.12 m
Max weight:	5,800 lb/2,631 kg (IA)
Max level speed:	307 knots/567 km/h (IA)
Power plant:	One 1,030 hp/768 kW Rolls-Royce Merlin II (IA)
Built by Westland:	685

As World War II progressed, attacks from high altitude bombers became a major problem. To combat this, Air Ministry Specification F4/40 was drawn up calling for a suitable fighter, capable of operating above 40,000ft. In order to achieve this it was necessary to introduce cabin pressurisation and to design a large twin engine aircraft with the fuel and handling qualities for prolonged operation at high altitude.

At the time, the two prototypes were projected to cost £104,000 each, demonstrating the aircraft's complexity, with production costs reducing significantly. Westland was awarded the contract for the Welkin (from the old English meaning 'sky' or 'heavens'). Despite considerable production numbers, the bombing threat did not materialise and the Welkin was used primarily for testing radar and cabin pressure systems.

The pioneering work on the Welkin resulted in Westland becoming a design authority on cabin systems and led directly to the foundation of Normalair Ltd as a subsidiary company, wholly concerned with cabin conditioning.

First flight:	1st November 1942
Span:	70 ft 0 in/21.34 m
Length:	41 ft 6 in/12.67 m
Max weight:	19,775 lb/8,970 kg
Max level speed:	336 knots/622 km/h
Power plant:	Two 1,250 hp/932 kW Rolls-Royce Merlin 72/73
Built by Westland:	77

AgustaWestland
A Finmeccanica Company

WESTLAND 1915-2015

Supermarine Seafire (1943)

'Somewhere off Korea'

Artist: Ronald Wong GAvA

In 1942 Westland began the conversion of 213 Spitfire MkVBs to the Seafire MkIIC standard and soon afterwards the company became the design authority for all Merlin-engined Seafires. This involved co-operation with the Supermarine design office in developing the Seafire's folding wing, requiring solutions to a number of tricky engineering problems brought about by the relative thinness of the wing section.

To assist with the growing volume of work, Westland engaged the services of Cunliffe-Owen Aircraft, who became sub-contractors to Westland rather than Supermarine. The two companies jointly produced all the MkIII Seafires and all but six of the later MkXV and MkXVIII Seafires with Griffon engines, work on which continued for a short time after the war.

Following the outbreak of the Korean War, HMS Triumph was diverted to operations to try to stem the North Korean offensive. Seafires flew ground attack and combat air patrols from July until September 1950.

First flight:	4th January 1943
Span:	36 ft 10 in/11.23 m
Length:	29 ft 11 in/9.12 m
Max weight:	7,010 lb/3,180 kg (IIC)
Max level speed:	288 knots/533 km/h (IIC)
Power plant:	One 1,340 hp/999 kW Rolls-Royce Merlin 45/46 or one 1,640 hp/1,223 kW Rolls-Royce Merlin 32 (IIC)
Built by Westland:	1,372

First flight:	Early 1943
Span:	49 ft 2 in/14.98 m
Length:	39 ft 9 in/12.11 m
Max weight:	13,068 lb/5,927 kg (I)
Max level speed:	204 knots/378 km/h (I)
Power plant:	One 1,260 hp/9,329 kW Rolls-Royce Merlin 30 (I)
Built by Westland:	5 (I) and 13 (II)

A carrier-borne, three seat torpedo and dive bomber, the Barracuda was developed as a replacement for the Fairey Aviation Company Ltd's Swordfish bomber. The type played a role in operations against the German battleship Tirpitz. Westland was initially contracted to build 250 Barracudas, but with Spitfire and Seafire production taking priority, this order was reduced to 18 which were built at Westland's wartime dispersal sites including one in Chard. Shown wearing roundels of the Pacific theatre during World War II, the Barracuda was flown from Royal Navy carriers. Although there are no surviving whole airframes, the Fleet Air Arm Museum is managing a project to restore a single static airframe from the remains of several crashed aircraft.

AgustaWestland
A Finmeccanica Company

WESTLAND 1915-2015

Westland Wyvern (1946)

'Wyverns over HMS Eagle'

Artist: Chris French GAvA

The requirement for the Wyvern was put forward in 1944 as Admiralty Specification N11/44, calling for a high performance long range fighter. The Mk1 was to use the large and powerful Rolls-Royce Eagle piston engine with contra-rotating propellers. The development was protracted and included several accidents, largely due to the complex engine/propeller combination. Production did proceed somewhat prematurely, as the piston engine variant never actually entered service.

It was decided that the Wyvern would benefit from the installation of one of the new turboprop engines. Two were available: the Rolls-Royce Clyde and the Armstrong Siddeley Python. Both units were tested and the Python was selected. The programme continued to be beset with problems and it was not until 1953 that the first Wyverns entered service.

Involved in Operation Musketeer, the Suez Crisis in 1956, Wyverns operated from HMS Eagle in the Mediterranean.

First flight:	12th December 1946 (TF Mk1), 22nd March 1949 (TF Mk2)
Span:	44 ft 0 in/13.41 m
Length:	39 ft 3 in/11.96 m
Max weight:	19,194 lb/8,706 kg
Max level speed:	333 knots/616 km/h
Power plant:	One 2,690 hp/2,006 kW Rolls-Royce Eagle 22 (TF Mk1), one 4,110 hp/3,065 kW Armstrong Siddeley Python (TF Mk2, T Mk3, S Mk4)
Built by Westland:	13 (TF Mk1) and 111 (TF Mk2)

Westland's first venture into helicopters was the Sikorsky S-51, adapted by the company to UK standards and called the Westland Dragonfly. Anglicisation included the introduction of the Alvis Leonides engine and the use of British specification materials.

Versions were produced for the Royal Navy, the RAF and civil operators. Those for the Royal Navy were equipped for sea rescue and communication duties, while those for the RAF were primarily equipped for casualty evacuation. Rescue versions carried a hoist capable of lifting 375lb (170 kg). The Dragonfly entered service with 705 NAS at RNAS Gosport in 1950 and was used extensively in Malaya by the RAF.

The painting shows a Dragonfly from 705 NAS, flown by Lt R Turpin, flying over the Zealand area of Holland, after a combination of gale force winds and spring tides on 31st January 1953. The floods caused over 1,300 people to drown and extensive damage. The squadron operated over the area searching for survivors and making numerous rescues from the flooding. Lt Turpin also had the honour of flying HM Queen Juliana of the Netherlands on a tour of the flood damaged areas.

First flight:	5th October 1948
Rotor diameter:	48 ft 0 in/14.63 m
Length:	58 ft 1 in/17.72 m
Max weight:	5,900 lb/2,675 kg
Max speed:	90 knots/167 km/h
Power:	One 520 hp/388 kW Alvis Leonides 521/1
Built by Westland:	149

Westland Whirlwind (1952) and Westland Widgeon (1955)

Artist:
David Shepherd CBE FRSA FRGS VPGAvA
'Westland Paint Shop 1957'

WESTLAND WHIRLWIND

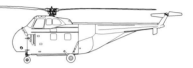

First flight:	12th November 1952
Rotor diameter:	53 ft 0 in/16.15 m
Length:	62 ft 1 in/18.94 m
Max weight:	7,500 lb/3,402 kg
Max speed:	95 knots/175 km/h
Power:	One 600 hp/447 kW Pratt & Whitney Wasp R-1340-40
Built by Westland:	446 (all marks)

WESTLAND WIDGEON

First flight:	23rd August 1955
Rotor diameter:	49 ft 2 in/14.99 m
Length:	58 ft 1 in/17.72 m
Max weight:	5,900 lb/2,675 kg
Max speed:	90 knots/167 km/h
Power:	One 520 hp/388 kW Alvis Leonides 521/1
Built by Westland:	15

After the Dragonfly had entered service, Westland announced that the agreement with Sikorsky had been extended to build the S-55 for the UK Armed Forces. The Westland-built version, the Whirlwind, was supplied to the RAF to operate in the rescue and transport roles. The Royal Navy used the aircraft for Search and Rescue and anti-submarine duties. Two Whirlwind HCC Mk8 aircraft were used by The Queen's Flight.

The Widgeon was Westland's first excursion into helicopter design, involving the major redesign of the S-51 (Westland Dragonfly) including an entirely new cabin and metal rotor blades. A new flying control system was incorporated and the centre of gravity range was improved by fitting a rotor head based on that of the Whirlwind to produce a five seat general purpose helicopter for the civil market. The first three aircraft were conversions, followed by a number of new-build machines.

The picture was painted inside the Bellman Hangar (now Building 137) on the Yeovil site which was the Paint Shop at the time. It is not certain whether the cat was a company mascot or was kept to keep the rodents at bay.

AgustaWestland
A Finmeccanica Company

The adoption of the Sikorsky S-58 and its complete redesign served to strengthen the Westland design team even further. The result was the Westland Wessex - a general purpose and anti-submarine helicopter using the Sikorsky S-58 airframe and transmission, modified to accept a turboshaft engine, full autopilot and Active Dipping Sonar for service with the Royal Navy. A number of Mk1 aircraft were adapted to operate in the Commando role.

First flight:	17th May 1957
Rotor diameter:	56 ft 0 in/7.07 m
Length:	65 ft 9 in/20.04 m
Max weight:	12,600 lb/5,715 kg
Max speed:	115 knots/212 km/h
Power:	One 1,450 shp/1,085 kW Napier Gazelle 13 Mk161 turboshaft
Built by Westland:	382 (all marks)

'Twenty Years Between: Wessex and Lysander'

Westland Westminster (1958)

'Transporting a Bridge Section'

Artist: Peter Sumpter GAvA

The Westminster extended the Westland helicopter design organisation once again in an attempt to produce a large single rotor transport helicopter. The project was based upon a research vehicle, wholly funded by Westland, using the Sikorsky S-56 rotor and transmission system, powered by two large Eland gas turbines. Two prototypes were produced. This painting represents the first which was a dedicated research airframe with a simple tubular steel structure.

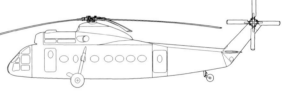

First flight:	15th June 1958
Rotor diameter:	72 ft 0 in/21.95 m
Length:	86 ft 9 in/26.44 m
Max weight:	33,000 lb/14,969 kg
Max speed:	130 knots/241 km/h
Power:	Two 3,150 shp/2,349 kW Napier Eland E229A turboshafts
Built by Westland:	2

AgustaWestland
A Finmeccanica Company

The second prototype was fully aerodynamically representative and was intended to lead to a production standard. However, indications were that official support could not be guaranteed and further work did not proceed beyond the research phase.

This painting shows the Westminster departing from White Waltham, a base of the Fairey Aviation Company Ltd, for the 1960 Farnborough Airshow. A Fairey Rotodyne is depicted on the ground.

At this time the helicopter industry in the UK was being rationalised. This rationalisation ultimately lead to the merger of Fairey's UK aviation interests, the helicopter division of the Bristol Aeroplane Company and Saunders-Roe into Westland Helicopters. This led to some of Westland's most notable products such as the Scout and the Wasp.

'Plucked From Hell'

Artist: Peter Sumpter GAvA

The installation of a single Rolls-Royce Gnome turboshaft engine into the Whirlwind airframe represented a considerable improvement on the basic S-55 from which it was derived. It was primarily used in the Search and Rescue role.

Here, a Whirlwind from 22 Squadron RAF is depicted conducting a rescue from FV Jeanne Gougy, a French trawler which ran aground and capsized off Land's End on 11th November 1962.

First flight:	28th February 1959
Rotor diameter:	53 ft 0 in/16.15 m
Length:	62 ft 1 in/18.94 m
Max weight:	7,800 lb/3,538 kg
Max speed:	95 knots/175 km/h
Power:	One 1,050 shp/783 kW Rolls-Royce Gnome H-1000 turboshaft

This five seat general purpose helicopter was the result of continued development of the Saunders-Roe P531 for the British Army. Design and manufacture of the Scout was the responsibility of the Fairey Division at Hayes. The Scout was the first helicopter in the British Army to be armed with an anti-tank missile, the SS-11, introducing the Army Air Corps to turbine-powered helicopters and helicopter anti-armour operations. It operated in the UK and Northern Ireland, the Middle East, Hong Kong, Brunei and the Falklands. It remained in service with the British Army until 1994.

As this image depicts, an aircraft that played a significant role in the Falklands conflict, and particularly in the evacuation of casualties, was the Westland Scout. It was flown by the Royal Marines and the British Army.

Westland Scout (1960)

'Eagle Patrols'

Artist: Mark Trueman AGAvA

The Scout deployed to Northern Ireland soon after the conflict began. Its ability to drop off patrols on narrow roads and in confined spaces ensured its suitability as a platform for the four man 'Eagle Patrols'. Later it was developed by Special Forces as a counter terrorist platform for assaults by abseiling down onto targets such as the roofs of buildings and the wings of hijacked airliners before forcing an entry.

First flight:	4th August 1960
Rotor diameter:	32 ft 3 in/9.83 m
Length:	40 ft 4 in/12.29 m
Max weight:	5,300 lb/2,404 kg
Max speed:	114 knots/211 km/h
Power:	One 1,050 shp/783 kW Rolls-Royce Nimbus 101 turboshaft
Built by Westland:	163

The Wasp was developed to meet the Royal Navy's requirement for a five seat general purpose shipborne helicopter for operation from small ships such as frigates. The aircraft was based on the Scout airframe and was a direct result of earlier work carried out with the Saunders-Roe P531. It incorporated a central deck securing point that led to the development of the Lynx Harpoon System.

Alongside the Wessex HAS Mk3, Wasps from HMS Antrim, Brilliant and Plymouth disabled the Argentinian submarine Sante Fe on 25th April 1982. In addition to the aircraft produced for the Royal Navy, the Wasp served with the naval forces of the Netherlands, South Africa, New Zealand, Brazil, Indonesia and Malaysia.

First flight:	28th October 1962
Rotor diameter:	32 ft 3 in/9.83 m
Length:	40 ft 4 in/12.29 m
Max weight:	5,500 lb/2,495 kg
Max speed:	104 knots/193 km/h
Power:	One 1,050 shp/783 kW Rolls-Royce Nimbus 103 turboshaft
Built by Westland:	134

WESTLAND 1915-2015

Westland Wasp (1962)

'Circles'

Artist: Chris French GAvA

This painting shows a Westland Wasp in the hover over the flight deck off the port beam of HMS Leander. The Wasp served on the Royal Navy's Leander and Rothesay class frigates, as well as the ice patrol vessel HMS Endurance.

'Del Boy'   Artist: Rob Hames AGAvA

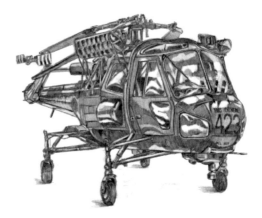

Westland Wasp HAS Mk1, XT437, was delivered to the Royal Navy in November 1965 and served with 829 NAS aboard Leander class frigate HMS Diomede. Nicknamed 'Del Boy', it took part in the 1976 'Cod War' against Icelandic fishing vessels. It was later transferred to the Aeroplane & Armament Experimental Establishment, Boscombe Down, to research lightning strikes upon helicopter airframes. It is now in the Boscombe Down Aviation Collection at Old Sarum.

WESTLAND 1915-2015

AgustaWestland
A Finmeccanica Company

The later marks of Wessex were modified to accept two Rolls-Royce Gnome turboshaft engines. The twin engine Wessex, powered by the Bristol Siddeley (later Rolls-Royce) Gnome turbines, proved to be one of Westland's most successful and enduring aircraft. The type served with the RAF (HC Mk2), the Royal Navy (HU Mk5) and a number were still in service in 1998 including the two with The Queen's Flight (designated HCC Mk4). A version was also produced for the civil market, known as the Wessex 60. This painting shows the Wessex HC Mk2 from the Newark Air Museum collection.

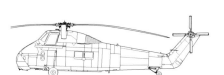

First flight:	18th January 1962
Rotor diameter:	56 ft 0 in/17.07 m
Length:	65 ft 9 in/20.04 m
Max weight:	12,600 lb/5,715 kg
Max speed:	115 knots/212 km/h
Power:	Two 1,350 shp/1,007 kW Bristol Siddeley Gnome Mk110/111 turboshafts

Westland Wessex HC Mk2 (1962)

Artist: David John Rowlands AGAvA

The painting shows the Wessex HC Mk2 operating in Northern Ireland in September 1985 where it served with 72 Squadron RAF from 1969 to 2002, almost throughout that period of conflict. It depicts a Royal Engineers patrol deploying by Wessex when a suspicious device was found with specialist equipment and a dog handler.

The Wessex was a familiar sight being escorted out of Bessbrook Mill helicopter landing site by a Gazelle or Lynx of the Army Air Corps and operating alongside the Sea King from the Royal Navy over South Armagh. Indeed Westland built all eight types of helicopter that were permanently based in Northern Ireland to support UK Armed Forces operations from August 1969 to July 2007.

'Search Party Reaction. Wessex HC Mk2 helicopter at Bessbrook Mill, South Armagh'

Designed by Bell Helicopter and made famous by its Medevac role in the Korean conflict, the British Army selected the Bell 47 or 'Sioux' in 1963 to fulfil light observation, communications and utility roles. Agusta and Westland delivered some 300 aircraft, starting with aircraft that were fully assembled by Agusta pending the availability of the Westland assembly line. After this, all aircraft were assembled in the UK from kits supplied by Agusta and the UK supply base. Most aircraft were designated as the 'Army Helicopter' or AH Mk1 but a small batch was designated as 'Helicopter Training' or HT Mk2 for training duties with the RAF.

A civil certified variant of the helicopter was built in small numbers and used by Bristow for training British Army pilots and by other civilian operators for general duties. The picture depicts the Sioux AH Mk1 of the Army Air Corps Helicopter Display Team, the Blue Eagles, training at Middle Wallop.

First flight:	March 1965
Rotor diameter:	37 ft 2 in/11.3 m
Length:	31 ft 7 in/9.63 m
Max weight:	2,950 lb/1,339 kg
Max speed:	91 knots/169 km/h
Power:	One 260 hp/210 kW Lycoming TVO-435-F1A
Built by Westland:	252

'Blue Eagles at Middle Wallop'

AgustaWestland
A Finmeccanica Company

WESTLAND 1915-2015

Westland Wessex HAS Mk3 (1965)

'Humphrey and Santa Fe'

Artist: Michael Turner FGAvA (President)

The Wessex Mk3 represented a substantial rework of the basic aircraft. Although it utilised the same airframe, the aircraft incorporated a sophisticated avionics system and Automatic Flight Control System. It is generally accepted that the Wessex Mk3 represents one of the first examples of an integrated avionics weapon system for anti-submarine duties. Most aircraft were conversions from the Mk1 standard.

The painting represents 'Humphrey' which is one of the most famous aircraft of the Falklands War. It embarked on HMS Antrim which was one of several ships sent to retake the islands of South Georgia. On 21st April 1982, in appalling weather conditions, Humphrey led two Wessex HU Mk5 helicopters to pick up Special Forces troops from the Fortuna Glacier above Grytviken. Using its radar to guide them through the storm, Humphrey led the helicopters but blizzard conditions caused the other helicopters to crash as they tried to take off from the glacier, forcing Humphrey to make a return trip to rescue all the troops and crew.

On the 25th April Humphrey spotted the Argentinian submarine Santa Fe on the surface and attacked it with depth charges which damaged the submarine. Helicopters from other ships joined the attack with torpedoes and AS12 missiles, causing Santa Fe to be abandoned.

In May, during the landings on the main Falkland Islands, HMS Antrim was strafed by Argentinian Dagger fighters which damaged Humphrey with splinters from cannon shells. These holes were patched with tape and Humphrey continued to fly. The aircraft is now in the Fleet Air Arm Museum at RNAS Yeovilton with many holes still visible.

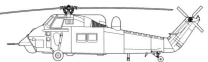

First flight:	August 1965
Rotor diameter:	56 ft 0 in/17.07 m
Length:	65 ft 9 in/20.04 m
Max weight:	13,600 lb/6,181 kg
Max speed:	120 knots/222 km/h
Power:	One 1,600 shp/1,193 kW Napier Gazelle 165

WESTLAND 1915-2015

AgustaWestland
A Finmeccanica Company

Westland undertook to build the Sikorsky SH-3D under licence as the Sea King. The Westland version included several modifications to improve its use in the anti-submarine role and was also subsequently adapted for Search and Rescue, Commando and Airborne Early Warning roles. Four airframes were purchased from Sikorsky and modified to the British standard to take Rolls-Royce Gnome engines, with electronic fuel systems and a comprehensive avionics fit, including radar.

The first Sea King HAS Mk1 entered service with the Royal Navy in 1969 and the type has continued to serve in the anti-submarine role with a number of upgrades as HAS Mk2, Mk5 and Mk6. The Sea King HAR Mk3/3A operated by the RAF first flew in 1977. This painting depicts a typical rescue by these iconic yellow helicopters which, alongside the Search and Rescue Mk5 of the Royal Navy, have captured the hearts of the British public for over 35 years.

First flight:	7th May 1969
Rotor diameter:	62 ft 0 in/18.9 m
Length:	72 ft 8 in/22.15 m
Max weight:	21,400 lb/9,707 kg
Max speed:	113 knots/209 km/h
Power:	Two 1,500 shp/1,119 kW Rolls-Royce Gnome 1400 turboshafts
Built By Westland:	330 (all marks)

AgustaWestland
A Finmeccanica Company

WESTLAND 1915-2015

Westland-Aérospatiale Gazelle (1970)

Artist: John Young VPGAvA VPASAA

In the 1960s there was a UK Armed Forces requirement for a range of new helicopters which was met, following the Anglo-French Helicopter Agreement in 1967, through a collaboration with French company Aerospatiale to produce three new designs: the Puma, Gazelle and Lynx.

The Gazelle was ordered to provide a Light Observation Helicopter for the Army Air Corps and a basic trainer for all the UK Armed Forces. All the aircraft destined for the UK were built by Westland, although design authority has remained Aérospatiale. A small number of Gazelles for civil use were also built.

The painting depicts a Gazelle in the hover over Belfast, Northern Ireland where it flew many thousands of hours in support of the security forces during that period of conflict. It was painted in 1994 to commemorate 25 years of continuous operations by the Army Air Corps in Northern Ireland. In the background a Westland Sioux can be seen returning to Sydenham Airfield where it was first deployed in 1969.

First flight:	28th April 1970
Rotor diameter:	34 ft 6 in/10.5 m
Length:	39 ft 2 in/11.94 m
Max weight:	3,747 lb/1,700 kg
Max speed:	167 knots/310 km/h
Power:	One 590 shp/440 kW Turbomeca Astazou IIIA turboshaft
Built by Westland:	294

'665 Sqn AAC Gazelle over Belfast - 1994'

Westland took design leadership for the Lynx, while Aerospatiale were responsible for the Puma and Gazelle. Both companies took part in the development and manufacture of all the aircraft. Westland was responsible for around 30% of the Puma airframe and some components, as well as the final assembly and flight testing of the 48 aircraft for the RAF.

The Puma entered service with the RAF as a medium transport helicopter in 1971.

First flight:	25th November 1970
Rotor diameter:	49 ft 2 in/15.00 m
Length:	59 ft 8 in/18.18 m
Max weight:	14,110 lb/6,400 kg
Max speed:	151 knots/280 km/h
Power:	Two 1,320/984 kW Turbomeca Turmo III C4 turboshafts
Built by Westland:	48

Westland Lynx (1971)

'The First Lynx in Spring'

Artist: David Gibbings MBE

The third helicopter of the Anglo-French Agreement was the Westland WG13 which was to become the Lynx. The first development aircraft was the Army utility variant with the skid undercarriage which eventually became the Lynx AH Mk1. This aircraft, XX153, quickly showed its pace and on 20th June 1972, flown by Roy Moxam, it set a new world speed record of 199.92mph over a 15-25 km course in the E1 class for helicopters.

First flight:	12th April 1971
Rotor diameter:	42 ft 0 in/12.8 m
Length:	49 ft 9 in/15.16 m
Max weight:	8,500 lb/3,863 kg
Max speed:	140 knots/259 km/h
Power:	Two 1,120 shp/835 kW Rolls-Royce Gem 41-1 turboshafts
Built by Westland:	432 (all marks)

WESTLAND 1915-2015

AgustaWestland
A Finmeccanica Company

The naval variant of the Lynx was designed to provide a small ships helicopter for the Royal Navy and the French Navy, capable of operating in the anti-surface vessel and anti-submarine roles and working from the decks of small ships such as frigates and destroyers. The first naval Lynx entered service with the Royal Navy in September 1976.

In 1989 the first Lynx HAS Mk8 was extensively modified to include the introduction of a computer-controlled Central Tactical System, high technology blades and increased take-off weight. The resultant Mk8 represented the first step towards the Super Lynx which included a 'glass cockpit', 360° radar, FLIR and the later CTS800 engine.

The painting shows a typical Cold War scene of a Royal Navy Lynx executing a close encounter with a Soviet Navy ship.

WESTLAND 1915-2015

Westland 30 (1979)

In 1976 Westland began to examine a larger private venture helicopter as the next progressive stage from the Lynx. Designated WG30 it embodied an almost unchanged Lynx engine, transmission and rotor system with a much larger rectangular cross-section fuselage. British Airways Helicopters purchased three of the basic Series 100 variant which were delivered in 1982. Further orders from the US and India followed.

In 1983 and 1986 the Series 200 and 300 variants were produced. The main intention was to submit the design as a response to the requirement for a possible successor to the Puma and Wessex. It was also hoped that there would be a wide civil and military export market but sales did not materialise. In the event only one prototype of each was produced.

G-OGAS was the eighth Series 100 built and was operated from Beccles by British Airways Helicopters during the early 1980s to support gas rigs in the southern sector of the North Sea. The artist, a former Westland employee, was the Flight Test Engineer aboard G-OGAS for its first flight on 18th April 1983.

First flight:	10th April 1979
Rotor diameter:	43 ft 8 in/13.31 m
Length:	52 ft 2 in/15.9 m
Max weight:	12,800 lb/5,806 kg
Max speed:	130 knots/241 km/h
Power:	Two 1,120 shp/835 kW Rolls-Royce Gem 42-1 turboshafts
Built by Westland:	40

WESTLAND 1915-2015

AgustaWestland
A Finmeccanica Company

The first order for the Lynx Mk88 was placed by the West German Navy in 1980 and eventually 19 aircraft were delivered. Graf Zeppelin 83+02 of German Navy Squadron MFG-3 is shown launching from the deck of the frigate FGS Bremen in the Baltic Sea during the 1980s. The naval variants of the Lynx have been one of the most successful exports produced at Yeovil. During its service with the armed services of 17 nations across the world its reputation grew and it earned the accolade of "the world's best small ship helicopter".

The Lynx naval variant is still being manufactured in 2015 and has been sold to Algeria, Argentina, Brazil, Denmark, France, Germany, South Korea, the Netherlands, Nigeria, Malaysia, Norway, Oman, Pakistan, Portugal, South Africa, Thailand and the UK.

Westland Sea King AEW Mk2A (1982) & Mk7 ASaC (2001)

Artist: Ronald Wong GAvA

'Sea King Mk7 ASaC Over Helmand'

One of the most important Westland Sea King developments resulted from an Urgent Operational Requirement during the Falklands War following the loss of HMS Sheffield, a Type 42 destroyer, as the result of a direct hit by a sea-skimming Exocet missile launched from an Argentinian Super Etendard aircraft. Working in partnership with the Royal Navy and Thorn EMI Electronics in a programme known as Project LAST (Low Altitude Surveillance Task) an Airborne Early Warning (AEW) capability was developed in only eight weeks and was designated the Sea King AEW Mk2.

Although the conflict had ended, the aircraft embarked on HMS Illustrious in August 1982 to provide initial airborne early warning for the British naval vessels within the 200 mile radius total exclusion zone surrounding the Falklands.

This painting depicts the ASaC Mk7 (Airborne Surveillance and Control), an upgraded version based around the Searchwater 2000 AEW radar. The Sea King Mk7 deployed to Afghanistan in May 2009 to watch the movement of vehicles and suspect targets, demonstrating its ability to switch roles and operate in land-based counter insurgency operations.

WESTLAND 1915-2015

AgustaWestland
A Finmeccanica Company

The painting depicts the calm, hazy evening of 11th August 1986. A Lynx helicopter, flown by Westland's Chief Test Pilot, Trevor Egginton, was fitted with Westland's high technology rotor blades and flew a course across the Somerset levels achieving an average speed of 249.10 mph (216.46 knots 400.87 km/h). In doing so it became the world's fastest helicopter, a record which remains unbroken. Although the helicopter had undergone a short modification programme to provide the power and control to make it capable of such speeds, the basic airframe and rotor transmission were unchanged from that of the Lynx helicopter in service worldwide.

David Gibbings was the Deputy Chief Flight Test Engineer at the time and as an artist and engineer he was able to depict the moment the record was taken.

AgustaWestland
A Finmeccanica Company

WESTLAND 1915-2015

Westland WS-70 Black Hawk (1987)

'Black Hawk on the Move"

CGI Artist: David Jacklin

A direct result of company's association with Sikorsky during the 1980s, after the period known as 'The Westland Affair', was an agreement that Westland would build approximately 90 Black Hawk helicopters under licence for supply to Saudi Arabia under the 'Al Yamamah' programme. Although a single aircraft was assembled from a kit provided by Sikorsky and flown successfully, the order did not materialise nor did the Black Hawk fulfil the requirements of the UK MoD. Events had been overtaken by the outbreak of the Gulf War, after which the requirements changed.

First Flight:	1st April 1987
Rotor diameter:	53 ft 8 in/16.36 m
Length:	63 ft 8 in/19.76 m
Max weight:	22,000 lb/9,979 kg
Max speed:	158 knots/293 km/h
Power:	Two 1,870 shp/1,394 kW General Electric T-700-GE-701C turboshafts
Built by Westland:	1

AgustaWestland
A Finmeccanica Company

The EH101 programme was launched in 1980 by the formation of European Helicopter Industries to manage the co-ordinated activities of Westland and Agusta in producing a replacement for the Sea King, with potential for worldwide sales in all appropriate roles. This major programme required nine prototypes and resulted in the EH101 and later AW101 series of aircraft. The programme had a much wider impact as it was a major factor leading to the merger of the two companies to create AgustaWestland.

The Merlin HM Mk1 was the UK maritime variant of the EH101. The UK MoD selected the name 'Merlin' from employee submissions. Alternatives had included 'Kingfisher' and 'Phoenix'. In Canada, the Search and Rescue variant is known as the 'Cormorant'. It entered service with the Royal Navy as an anti-submarine warfare weapons system. An order for 44 Merlin Mk1s was placed for the Royal Navy.

Thirty Merlin Mk1s are currently being modernised to Mk2 standard which includes modernising the avionics and extending the capabilities to include casualty evacuation, troop transport and underslung loads. It remains the most advanced anti-submarine helicopter in the world, with a formidable array of fully integrated electronic processing, capable of operating from small ships using a similar deck securing system to that employed for the Lynx.

First flight:	9th October 1987
Rotor diameter:	61 ft 0 in/18.60 m
Length:	74 ft 10 in/22.81 m
Max weight:	32,188 lb/14,600 kg
Max speed:	167 knots/309 km/h
Power:	Three 2,100 shp/1,565 kW Rolls-Royce/ Turbomeca RTM322 turboshafts
Built by Westland:	186 (all marks, currently in production)

AgustaWestland
A Finmeccanica Company

Westland Sea King Mk43B (1989)

'Tryyg Havet'

Artist: Ronald Wong GAvA

In December 1970 an order was received for ten Sea Kings, designated Mk43, for use by the Royal Norwegian Air Force in the Search and Rescue role. The aircraft build standard was based on a previous order for the West German Navy. The first of these aircraft flew on 19th May 1972 and went into service in November after the first three aircraft had been delivered. In August 1989 Westland received an order to update the aircraft which included the modernisation of the navigation and communications equipment and the installation of FLIR and dual radar systems. This was designated the Mk43B. 'Trygg Havet', the motto of 330 Squadron Royal Norwegian Air Force translates as 'Guarding the Seas'.

The Sea King has also been delivered to Australia, Belgium, Egypt, Germany, India, Pakistan and Qatar and many are still flying in 2015.

In the late 1980s the British Army of the Rhine, facing Soviet forces across the inner German border, developed new tactics that required airmobile forces to conduct highly mobile 'counter-stroke' operations against massed armoured forces. This required an increase in the size of the British Army's light utility fleet and the decision was made in 1987 to build 16 new Lynx and convert eight existing Lynx AH Mk1 airframes with a new rugged-wheeled version of the battlefield variant of the Lynx. Designated the Lynx Mk9, the first prototype flew in 1989 and deliveries started in 1991. Two new British Army squadrons were formed, 672 and 673 Squadrons Army Air Corps, to support the 24th Airmobile Brigade.

These aircraft were soon deployed to the Balkans where they played a key role in the peace support operations during the 1990s.

EH Industries Merlin HC Mk3 (1996)

'Merlin the Magician'

Artist: Alex Hamilton GAvA

The Merlin Mk3 incorporated the rear door ramp configuration and provided a medium-sized battlefield support helicopter for the RAF with an initial order for 22 aircraft. The first of these aircraft entered service in January 2001 with 28 Squadron RAF based at RAF Benson.

The Merlin's first operational deployment was to the Balkans in 2003. In 2004 it was deployed to Iraq, supporting coalition forces in the Medevac role. The painting shows an RAF Merlin being escorted by a Lynx Mk7 in the area around Basra, where they operated until Britain's withdrawal in June 2009.

When the UK Armed Forces were operating simultaneously in both Iraq and Afghanistan there was considerable pressure on UK helicopter resources. To alleviate this six AW101s were acquired from Denmark in 2007 and converted to Merlin HC Mk3A standard. The HC Mk3As were used for training, allowing more Merlin Mk3s to be deployed in Afghanistan.

WESTLAND 1915-2015

AgustaWestland

A Finmeccanica Company

Early in the 1990s the British Army stated a requirement for an attack helicopter. Westland responded by negotiating a licence agreement to build the McDonnell Douglas (now Boeing) AH-64D Apache. The WAH-64 differed from the US aircraft by the introduction of the Rolls-Royce Turbomeca RTM322 and UK specific equipment. The first eight aircraft were built and test flown in the United States by Boeing and the remaining 59 were assembled in Yeovil.

The Westland-built Apache entered service with the British Army in 2000 and was deployed to Afghanistan, operating continuously from 2004 to 2014. The picture shows the Apache operating from HMS Ocean from which it launched air strikes into Libya during the conflict in 2013.

First flight:	25th September 1998
Rotor diameter:	48 ft 0 in/14.63 m
Length:	58 ft 3 in/17.76 m
Max weight:	21,000 lb/9,545 kg
Max speed:	160 knots/296 km/h
Power:	Two 2,100 shp/1,565 kW Rolls-Royce/ Turbomeca RTM322 turboshafts
Built by Westland:	59

Westland Apache AH Mk1 (1998)

'Apache Air and Ground Crew'

Artist: Richard Foster

Increasingly, AgustaWestland has provided a training service for aircrew, groundcrew and maintainers when an aircraft type is sold. When the British Army introduced the Apache into service, Westland, in partnership with Boeing, was contracted to provide a full training service for all the Army Air Corps personnel operating and maintaining the aircraft. This painting depicts the close working relationship between the ground and air crews of an Apache.

The AW101, manufactured in both the UK and Italy, has been exported to Algeria, Canada, Denmark, Japan, Norway, Nigeria, Portugal, Turkmenistan and sales are ongoing worldwide. It has been used in a number of ways, notably for Search and Rescue and more recently as a VVIP aircraft for governments and Heads of State.

This picture commemorates a rescue by Flyvevåbnet, the Royal Danish Air Force, on 8th January 2008, when Rescue 504 was scrambled from Skrydstrup to Rønne (Bornholm) for a PATEVAC (Patient Evacuation) mission in severe weather conditions. On the return journey, with the addition of a patient and nurse and halfway to Copenhagen, Rescue 504 responded to a MAYDAY call and quickly located and rescued two fishermen from their sinking vessel before resuming its mission. The success of this challenging operation in darkness and adverse weather is typical of the conditions in which the AW101 is able to operate as a Search and Rescue platform. It is also a tribute to the skill and courage displayed by the Royal Danish Air Force since its formation in 1960.

AgustaWestland
A Finmeccanica Company

WESTLAND 1915-2015

AgustaWestland Lynx AH Mk9A (2009)

Artist: Alex Hamilton GAvA

'*Lynx Over Dishforth*'

The Lynx Mk9A was similar to the Lynx Mk9 but with upgraded engines and a semi-digital glass cockpit. The aircraft was delivered as an Urgent Operational Requirement to the British Army in order to provide year-round performance in the hot and high conditions of Afghanistan. The programme saw the entire fleet of 22 Mk9 aircraft being modified to Mk9A standard over a three year period from November 2008 to November 2011. The first four Mk9As were deployed to Afghanistan by 9 Regiment Army Air Corps in April 2010 and the aircraft was regarded as a highly versatile asset and genuine force multiplier during this conflict.

In the background of the picture is the Lynx Mk7 which was generally similar to the basic variant but its improved performance extended its capabilities to include anti-armour operations equipped with anti-tank missiles. Modifications included improved cockpit management systems, a reversed-direction and more powerful tail rotor, composite blades which reduced noise and the ability to hover for extended periods at high weight, an important factor during anti-armour operations.

First flight:	September 2009 (Lynx Mk9A)
Rotor diameter:	42 ft 0 in/12.8 m
Length:	49 ft 9 in/15.16 m
Max weight:	11,750 lb/5,330 kg
Max speed:	160 knots/296 km/h
Power:	Two 1,621 shp/1,209 kW LHTEC CTS800-4N FADEC turboshafts
Built by AW:	22 Mk9 converted to Mk9A standard

The AW159 is built on the success of the Lynx family of helicopters. It resulted from the Future Lynx project, which would determine a replacement for the UK MoD's Lynx fleet. AgustaWestland's first aircraft to be entirely digitally designed, the AW159 has a new airframe, a state of the art avionics system and is designed to meet modern operational requirements. It has the capability to operate over both land and sea and can be easily converted between roles. It is now in service with the British Army and the Royal Navy, known as the Wildcat.

Artist: Alex Hamilton GAvA

'AW159 Wildcat HMA Mk2'

First flight:	12th November 2009
Rotor diameter:	42 ft 0 in/12.80 m
Length:	50 ft 0 in/15.24 m
Max weight:	13,227 lb/6,000 kg
Max speed:	150 knots/277 km/h
Power:	Two 1,361 shp/1,014 kW turboshafts with FADEC
Built by AW:	39 (currently in production)

AgustaWestland AW189 (2015)

'AW189 SAR – Search at First Light'

CGI Artist: Gary Weller

The AW189 is part of the AW Family of helicopters, which includes the AW169 and AW139. The Family concept includes a common design philosophy, whereby maintainers and crew can transition across platforms with relative ease.

Of these, only the AW189 is built in the UK and it is the first civil aircraft to be built here since the Westland 30. The AW189 is a brand new 8 tonne class twin engine helicopter which is designed to meet the need for a multirole, versatile and affordable platform. As such it is suited to long range, offshore transportation and Search and Rescue. In the Search and Rescue configuration, as seen here, the AW189 has capacity for up to four stretchers with eight seats.

This Computer Generated Image (CGI) is a typical example of media produced from three dimensional computer models which now cover the majority of AgustaWestland products. From these, customers are able to have a clear vision of their investment before the actual aircraft exists.

First flight:	24th January 2015 (UK-built)
Rotor diameter:	47 ft 11 in/14.60 m
Length:	57 ft 9 in/17.60 m
Max weight:	18,959 lb/8,600 kg
Max speed:	169 knots/313 km/h
Power:	Two 2,000 shp/1,491 kW General Electric CT7-2E1 Turboshafts with FADEC and one 60 kW APU
Built by AW:	1 (UK-built, currently in production)

WESTLAND 1915-2015

AgustaWestland
A Finmeccanica Company

'Wessex HU5 XS486'

ARTIST
BIOGRAPHIES

Artist: Christopher Draper AGAvA

A

B

C

TERRY AKEHURST

'Final Checks'
Westland Whirlwind

42

Terry Akehurst was born in 1938. From an early age he has felt the thrill and excitement of aeroplanes. Since his retirement from a career in aircraft engineering, he has pursued his lifelong enthusiasm for painting. A Friend of the Guild of Aviation Artists, he is self-taught and generally strives to achieve atmosphere and feeling in his work.

BARRY K BARNES GAvA

04

24

'Boys From Ark Royal'
Short 184

'Heat Haze'
Westland Wapiti

57 **'Evening Sunlight, Gibraltar'**
Westland Wasp

Barry Barnes became a member of the Guild of Aviation Artists in 1982. Working at RAF Kemble ignited his passion for aircraft. He is a self-taught artist who has a passion for drawing and painting, specialising in naval and aviation subjects as he enjoys the challenges these bring.

G P BRITNELL

'A Welkin in the Vault of Heaven'
Westland Welkin

46

Graham Britnell is a lifelong aviation enthusiast. He spent 28 years as an RAF airframe technician, observing his passion, before taking up painting to continue his love of aircraft. With no formal art background he considers himself a painter purely for leisure.

DAVID CALOW GAvA

'The Westland F7/30'
Westland F7/30

36

David Calow joined the Guild of Aviation Artists in 2004. He was elected Associate in 2006, Full Member in 2011 and has exhibited at the Annual Exhibition for nine years. Professionally he has over 30 years' experience as a designer and illustrator working in Leicester.

KAI CHOI AGAvA

27

30

34

'Westland Interceptor'
Westland F20/27 Interceptor

'Westland C.O.W. Gun Fighter'
Westland C.O.W. Gun Fighter

'Westland PV7'
Westland PV7

The flights around Hong Kong's Kai-Tak Airport were the catalyst for Kai Choi's interest in aviation and painting. Following engineering training, he studied technical illustration in London and freelanced for four years before pursuing music as a career. He resumed his aviation art in 2009 in parallel with his violin playing.

GRAHAM COOKE GAvA
(Chairman)

'Special Delivery'
Westland Lysander

39

Graham Cooke joined the RAF in 1962 as an Apprentice Airframe Fitter and subsequently served for 40 years as an Engineer, reaching the rank of Squadron Leader. He was made an MBE in the 1991 Gulf War Honours List. Always interested in art, he took up painting and framing full time on leaving the RAF and in 2009 was elected as Chairman of the Guild of Aviation Artists, a position which he continues to enjoy.

ANTHONY COWLAND FGAvA

iV

10

'The Ride Back to Bastion'
Westland Lynx

'Travellers'
Airco DH9A

65 **'Let Us Be Known By Our Actions'**
Westland-Aérospatiale Puma

After a career in design and architecture Anthony Cowland became a full time artist and illustrator in 1989. He enjoys painting many and varied subjects including aviation.

PAUL CROCKER

06

16

'Dual in the Clouds'
Sopwith 1 ½ Strutter

'Pre-Flight Check'
Westland Walrus

Paul Crocker was born in Margate in 1976 and apart from time serving in the armed forces as an Infantry Soldier and a year backpacking, has always lived in Kent. A Friend of the Guild of Aviation Artists, he tries to create an evocative image that tells a story.

JOHN PETER CUTTS AGAvA

44

75

'Spitfire MkVC Clipped Wing'
Supermarine Spitfire

'Rapid Reaction Croatia 1995, Lynx Utility'
Westland Lynx

John Peter Cutts was born in 1936 and studied at Sutton & Cheam School of Art. His interest in aviation began when he joined the ATC. He completed National Service between 1956-58 in the Army Air Corps in Malaya. John's career path took him into creative advertising and marketing, where he was the MD of Centrum Design Ltd. Since retiring he paints daily for pleasure and commissions. His other interests include social history and antiques.

D

RODNEY DIGGENS GAvA

'Wayward Westland'
Westland Limousine III

15

Born in August 1937 in South London, Rodney Diggens studied at Camberwell School of Arts and Crafts followed by a varied career in advertising and printing. A successful move to work freelance followed with a range of clients including BAe, IPC, Sun Alliance and a number of agencies and private individuals.

JOHN DIMOND GAvA

'Wessex Six Seater'
Westland IV

'Wessex Eight Seater'
Westland IV

28

John Dimond's love of painting and lifelong fascination with flying led to specialisation in aviation art. Accepted into the Guild of Aviation Artists in 1980, John has enjoyed a wide range of subject matter, exhibited in municipal and private galleries throughout the world.

29

CHRISTOPHER DRAPER AGAvA

'Wessex HU5 XS486'
Westland Wessex

Christopher Draper is an illustrator and artist living in Wiltshire. After training as an architect and a few years in practice he made the decision to concentrate on painting full time. Now he splits his time between architectural, aviation and historical subjects.

83

F

JAMES FIELD AGAvA

05

11

11

12

12

41

'Empress at Stavros 1916'
Short 166

'Westland Wagtail'
Westland Wagtail

'Westland Weasel'
Westland Weasel

'Wagtail v Snail v Wasps'
Westland Wagtail

'Weasel v Badger v Dragonfly'
Westland Weasel

'263 Squadron Rhubarb 19-10-43'
Westland Whirlwind

James Field has worked as an illustrator and artist for over 30 years having attended art college in the late 1970s-1980s. His subjects have included dinosaurs, wildlife and history, especially military, samurai and aviation. His books and paintings have been sold across the world.

PATRICIA FORREST GAvA

'Secret Rendezvous'
Westland Lysander

40

After leaving the Royal College of Art Patricia Forrest worked as a freelance graphic designer. She joined the Guild in 1987 and became a Full Member in 1994. Apart from commissions, for the last ten years she has worked for the RAF Charitable Trust, amongst others, producing many aviation paintings each year for publication.

RICHARD FOSTER

'Apache Air and Ground Crew'
Westland Apache AH Mk1

78

Richard Foster was born in London and brought up in Norfolk. He was educated at Harrow School, Trinity College Oxford and Studio Simi in Florence. He is a Member of the Royal Society of Portrait Painters and is principally a painter of portraits, landscapes and figurative work. He has staged ten one-man exhibitions since 1978.

CHRIS FRENCH GAvA

'Wyverns over HMS Eagle'
Westland Wyvern

'Circles'
Westland Wasp

48

Chris French GAvA is a Full Member of the Guild of Aviation Artists. He has specialised in aviation for 25 years but has covered many other subjects in his paintings. He has exhibited at the RAF Museum, Fleet Air Arm Museum and USAF Museum in Dayton, Ohio as

58

well as various galleries and has won many awards including the UK's prestigious 'Aviation Painting of the Year'. Chris researches his subjects thoroughly and likes to create dynamic and interesting images that tell a story.

G

ROY GARNER GAvA

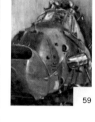

31

59

67

'Pterodactyl IV'
Westland Pterodactyl IV

'Newark's Wessex'
Westland Wessex

'David & Goliath'
Westland Lynx

Roy Garner studied at the Warwickshire College of Art, Coventry College of Art, obtained the City & Guilds final in Illustration and formed a studio lasting ten years. Employed by Jaguar as an artist, he retired in 2005 and has a PPL with over 2,000 hours flying experience. He joined the Guild in 1991 and became a Full Member in 1997.

DAVID GIBBINGS MBE

'The First Lynx in Spring'
Westland Lynx

'Putting the Record Straight'
Westland Lynx

66

David Gibbings was a founding member of the Guild and one of their most active advocates and supporters. He was responsible for establishing the Agus-

71

taWestland trophy and judges annually. As a lifelong Flight Test Engineer he retired as Chief FTE of AgustaWestland in 1993. An ex-RAF engineer and later navigator, he has been involved in flight operations and flight testing for over 50 years.

H

ROB HAMES AGAvA

'Del Boy'
Westland Wasp

58

Growing up under Wiltshire's skies, full of aircraft, soon fused with Rob Hames's artistic side, creating a passion for aviation art and in particular the aircraft of Boscombe Down. Teaching art for several years lead to a thorough approach and at present he is an Associate of the Guild of Aviation Artists.

ALEX HAMILTON GAvA

76

80

'Merlin The Magician'
Merlin

'Lynx Over Dishforth'
Westland Lynx

'AgustaWestland AW159 Wildcat HMA Mk2'
AW159 Wildcat

81

Alex Hamilton is a professional aviation artist, being a commercial illustrator until 2000, when he took up aviation painting full time. He is a Full Member of the Guild of Aviation Artists and has been awarded 'Painting of The Year' on two occasions at the Guild's Annual Exhibition at the Mall Galleries, London.

H

NEIL HIPKISS AGAvA

'Merlin Mk2 Royal Navy'
EH Industries EH101
Merlin

Neil Hipkiss is an established artist specialising in private, commercial and military aviation art with a particular interest in modern military aircraft. His preferred choice of medium is oils on stretched canvas. His paintings hang in prestigious corporate and private collections around the world, such as the RAF Club.

BRIAN HOW AGAvA

'Westland Yeovil'
Westland Yeovil

Brian How served in the Metropolitan Police for 34 years, retiring as an Inspector. He moved from London to Stoke sub Hamdon in 2006. His father served in Bomber Command during World War II. His brother served in the RAF as well as his nephew who is currently a Flight Sergeant helicopter engineer. He has always painted but aviation art took over when he joined the Guild of Aviation Artists.

J

DAVID JACKLIN

'Black Hawk on the Move'
Westland WS70 Black Hawk

David Jacklin is a Graphics and Illustration Specialist with a background in aviation illustration stretching back to the 1980s when he worked for CASA in Madrid, Spain. He joined AgustaWestland in 1995 and since then has worked in the Bids, Marketing and Publicity departments creating a mixture of electronic and interactive artwork.

L

IEUAN LAYTON-MATTHEWS GAvA

'Whirlwind Raid at Dawn'
Westland Whirlwind

Ieuan Layton-Matthews was born in Cardiff in 1940. He attended Gowerton Boys Grammar School during 1950s. He studied at both Bath Academy Of Art in 1960-64 and the Institute Of Education University of London 1965. He taught art at Kettering Boys Grammar School 1966-1974 and later a lectured at Swansea Institute Arch. Glass Department in the 1980s. Ieuan joined the GAvA in 1998 and has exhibited annually to the present day.

DAVID LIVESLEY

'Westminster at White Waltham'
Westland Westminster

David Livesley has been an airport planner/designer for the last 30 years, working on airport expansion projects around the world. A lifelong aviation enthusiast and Friend of the Guild of Aviation Artists, he has been developing his interest in drawing and painting in recent years, exhibiting at the Guild's annual exhibition for the first time in 2014.

M

GEOFF MARSH AGAvA

'Westbury'
Westland Westbury

Geoff Marsh is a watercolour artist with 40 years' experience as a commercial artist. As well as aircraft he paints landscapes and animal portraits and won the Durham Open Art Competition in 2010. He lives with his wife and son in Castle Eden, County Durham.

SIMON MILAN GAvA

'The One that Wouldn't Fly'
C29

'CL20'
CL20

Simon Milan has had a lifelong interest in aviation matters. He studied A-level art at school (in the early 1960s) and discovered the Guild of Aviation Artists in the 1980s. This enabled him to combine his two key interests of art and aviation. He is a regular exhibitor at the Guild's Annual Exhibitions and is currently its Vice-Chairman.

C RUPERT MOORE

'Westland Widgeon II G-EBRO'
Westland Widgeon

Educated at Doncaster Grammar School, C Rupert Moore attended the Royal College of Art and became a renowned stained glass designer, latterly working as a designer for Whitefriars. He also worked as an aeronautical artist and aero-modeller, both talents making him a household name to readers of The Aeromodeller during the 1940s.

NIGEL W MORRIS AGAvA

'An Early Morning Start for Sabena Feeder Liners'
Westland Wessex

Born in 1957 Nigel studied as a Graphic Designer and Illustrator. Whilst working in the industry he became a tutor in art and design for several colleges. After redundancy he decided to return to college to study for a Bachelor of Design and later a Cert Ed. Nigel is currently a freelance artist and teacher.

P

COLIN H PAINE AGAvA

'Test Flight'
Westland Pterodactyl V

35

Colin H Paine studied art and design, working on many magazines during his career in publishing. He was formerly Art Editor on Flight International and now paints full time. He has been a glider pilot for many years and recently trained towards a PPL on Tiger Moths at Cambridge.

MARTIN PERMAN AGAvA

'Westland Woodpigeon at Lympne 1924'
Westland Woodpigeon

'Testing the Witch'
Westland Witch

18

26

Martin Perman has been painting aviation subjects for 35 years, but in a much more focused way in the last five after a career in engineering design and technical sales. He enjoys using watercolour, pencil and acrylic to try to put the subject in harmony with its surroundings.

R

DAVID JOHN ROWLANDS AGAvA

'Search Party Reaction. Wessex HC Mk2 helicopter at Bessbrook Mill, South Armagh'
Westland Wessex

60

David John Rowlands was sketching soldiers and aircraft when he was a boy. Since 1985 he has been going on operations with the Armed Forces in order to do paintings for the Army and RAF. He aims to present a realistic record of the dramatic events of war, with accuracy always important.

S

PATRICK SADLER AGAvA

'Spell of Elegance'
Westland Wizard

22

Patrick Sadler was born in Great Wilbraham, Cambridgeshire in 1967. He works primarily in pencil and pen and ink. Interested in history and aviation, he finds inspiration in black and white atmospheric images, combining his training in technical illustration with artistic flair and an eye for detail to convey past events.

DAVID SCRUTTON AGAvA

'Duxford's DH9'
Airco DH9

08

Born in 1945, David Scrutton took up painting on retirement in 2000. A private pilot, he combined his two passions by joining the Guild of Aviation Artists and has regularly shown his work at the Annual Exhibition. Although he works principally in watercolour, David enjoys experimenting in other media.

DAVID SHEPHERD CBE FRSA FRGS VPGAvA

'Westland Paint Shop 1957'
Westland Whirlwind and Widgeon

'Twenty Years Between: Wessex and Lysander'
Westland Wessex

50

51

David Shepherd started his career as an aviation artist for the RAF who flew him to Kenya in 1960 and commissioned his first wildlife painting.

In 1984 the David Shepherd Wildlife Foundation was set up to focus David's own conservation efforts and to raise awareness and funds for wildlife conservation.

ROBIN SMITH GAvA

'We Will Not Fail You'
Westland Sea King

63

Robin Smith, working from his studio in Lincolnshire, has always been keen on art and aircraft. A keen model maker, past pilot and full time artist, Robin admits it is the ultimate 'job', with several famous people on his books. "I will paint until no longer able to do so".

PETER SUMPTER GAvA

09

52

54

81

'Patrolling the Grand Fleet'
Westland N1B

'Plucked From Hell'
Westland Whirlwind

'Transporting a Bridge Section'
Westland Westminster

'A Prowling Wildcat'
AW159 Wildcat

Peter Sumpter's career commenced as a technical illustrator before joining the RAF as a topographical model maker. Following 15 years as Chief Artist at GEC producing artists' impressions and cutaway illustrations of nuclear power stations, he became a freelance artist incorporating teaching, commissioned works and 14 solo exhibitions. A Member of the Guild of Aviation Artists, his work spans the spectrum of flight.

DOUGLAS SWALLOW GAvA

'Desert Rendezvous'
Hawker Audax

38

Douglas Swallow joined the Guild of Aviation Artists as a Friend in 1983 and was elected to Associate in 1993 before becoming a Full Member in 2001. He was well known for his aviation paintings and also painted commissions. He exhibited paintings in the Guild's Annual Exhibition for over 17 years.

T

MARK TRUEMAN AGAvA

'Eagle Patrols'
Westland Scout

As a boy Mark Trueman was influenced by his grandfather and uncle who were professional artists. After leaving school he attended Medway Art College, later becoming a printer and retoucher then onto specialist decorations. He has exhibited work with local art groups and the Guild of Aviation Artists for 25 years.

MICHAEL TURNER FGAvA
(President)

'First Over Everest'
Westland PV3 and PV6

'Blue Eagles at Middle Wallop'
Westland/Agusta-Bell Sioux AHMk1

'Humphrey and Santa Fe'
Westland Wessex

Michael Turner has been a professional artist since 1954. His enthusiasm for aviation and motor sport has always been his principle inspiration, and he has flown in a wide variety of service aircraft to gain first-hand experience for his aviation paintings. He also flies his own Chipmunk aircraft.

CHRIS TYLER AGAvA

'Risky Exploration'
Westland 30

'Lynx Mk88 - Baltic Sea Mid 1980s'
Westland Lynx

Chris Tyler completed an engineering apprenticeship with Hawker Siddeley Aviation and achieved a degree in Aeronautical Engineering. He joined Westland in the mid-1970s and became Chief Flight Test Engineer. He joined National Air Traffic Services during 1991. He has been a lifelong aviation enthusiast.

W

GARY WELLER

'AW189 SAR – Search at First Light'
AW189

Gary Weller is a 3D Modelling & Animation Specialist with a background of traditional airbrush and painting skills. He joined AgustaWestland in 1989 and since then has used 3D and 2D software to produce images and animations for marketing and engineering projects.

KEITH WOODCOCK FGAvA

'Westland Wapiti'
Westland Wapiti

'Westland Wallace'
Westland Wallace 501 Squadron

'Fairey Barracuda'
Fairey Barracuda

'Evacuating Casualties during the Falklands War'
Westland Scout AH Mk1

Keith Woodcock has been a full-time professional artist for over 30 years and has won 18 awards for his work on both sides of the Atlantic. His paintings have been commissioned by aircraft manufacturers, airlines, air forces, government departments, publishers and private clients worldwide.

RONALD WONG GAvA

'Somewhere Off Korea'
Supermarine Seafire

'Sea King Mk7 ASaC Over Helmand'
Westland Sea King

'Trygg Havet'
Westland Sea King

'The Apache Goes to Sea'
Westland Apache

'Rescue 504'
AW101

Ronald Wong is an independent painter whose work embraces a diversity of subject matter, both within and beyond aviation. Aviation is a childhood love which continues to have a special place in his work and has resulted in hundreds of paintings and prints. He lives and works in St Albans.

Y

DAVID YOUNG

'Dragonfly Over Dutch Floods'
Westland Dragonfly

David Young studied at Falmouth School of Art, and has been working as a freelance illustrator for the last 20 years. Although he has always had a great interest in aircraft and, in particular, aviation art, it's only recently that he has really begun to fulfil his ambition to become a recognised aviation artist. He is also a Friend of the Guild of Aviation Artists.

JOHN YOUNG VPGAvA VPASAA

'De Havilland DH4'
Airco DH4

'Vickers Vimy Over the Pyramids'
Vickers Vimy

'665 Sqn AAC Gazelle over Belfast - 1994'
Westland-Aérospatiale Gazelle

John Young has painted the aviation scene as a professional for 65 years. At the 50th anniversary of Westland he was commissioned by Harald Penrose to paint a picture of the Pterodactyl. He is a founder member of the GAvA, has been Chairman and is now a Vice-president of the Guild and the American Aviation Art Society.